OCCASIONAL PAPER 170

# The West African Economic and Monetary Union

## Recent Developments and Policy Issues

By a Staff Team led by Ernesto Hernández-Catá

and comprising
Christian A. François, Paul Masson, Pascal Bouvier,
Patrick Peroz, Dominique Desruelle,
and Athanasios Vamvakidis

INTERNATIONAL MONETARY FUND
Washington DC
1998

Production: IMF Graphics Section
Figures: In-Ok Yoon
Typesetting: Victor Barcelona

**Library of Congress Cataloging-in-Publication Data**

The West African Economic and Monetary Union : recent developments and
   policy issues / by a staff team led by Ernesto Hernández-Catá : and comprising Christian A. François . . . [et al.].
      p.    cm. — (Occasional paper, ISSN 0251-6365 ; no. 170)
   Includes bibliographical references (p. ).
   ISBN 1-55775-755-0

   1. Union économique et monétaire Ouest africaine.    2. Monetary policy—Africa, French-speaking West.    I.  Hernández-Catá, Ernesto.
II.  François, C.A. (Christian A.)    III. Series: Occasional paper (International Monetary Fund) ; no. 170.
HG1371.W47 1998
332.4′566′0966—dc21                                                    98-41360
                                                                        CIP

Price: US$18.00
(US$15.00 to full-time faculty members and
students at universities and colleges)

Please send orders to:
International Monetary Fund, Publication Services
700 19th Street, N.W., Washington, D.C. 20431, U.S.A.
Tel.: (202) 623-7430      Telefax: (202) 623-7201
E-mail: publications@imf.org
Internet: http://www.imf.org

recycled paper

# Contents

**Appendix**

**Figures**
**Section**

---

The following symbols have been used throughout this paper:

. . .   to indicate that data are not available;

n.a.   to indicate not applicable;

—   to indicate that the figure is zero or less than half the final digit shown, or that the item does not exist;

–   between years or months (e.g., 1994–95 or January–June) to indicate the years or months covered, including the beginning and ending years or months;

/   between years (e.g., 1994/95) to indicate a crop or fiscal (financial) year.

"Billion" means a thousand million.

Minor discrepancies between constituent figures and totals are due to rounding.

The term "country," as used in this paper, does not in all cases refer to a territorial entity that is a state as understood by international law and practice; the term also covers some territorial entities that are not states, but for which statistical data are maintained and provided internationally on a separate and independent basis.

# Preface

An IMF staff team visited Ouagadougou and Dakar during November 11–14, 1997, to hold policy discussions with senior officials of the Central Bank of West African States (BCEAO), the regional Banking Commission, and the Commission of the West African Economic and Monetary Union (WAEMU). The WAEMU representatives were headed by Moussa Touré, president of the commission, and those of the BCEAO by Governor Charles Konan Banny. The discussions focused on a review of recent performance and on key regional economic policy issues, including (1) an examination of the framework for monetary policy, (2) an assessment of the banking sector, (3) the introduction of a common external tariff, and (4) other specific regional issues.

Given the widening range of economic policies that have been formulated and implemented at the regional level since the ratification of the WAEMU treaty in August 1994, and in view of the special characteristics of the CFA franc zone, both IMF staff and country authorities believe that these periodic regional discussions, which are essential to complement bilateral surveillance and monitoring of IMF-supported programs, should be strengthened. Accordingly, as part of a move to a more formal and comprehensive dialogue with the regional institutions of the WAEMU, annual reports on these discussions will be presented to the IMF's Executive Board.

The authors are grateful to many colleagues in the IMF for helpful comments on previous drafts. They would like to thank Ngoc Lê for her valuable assistance in preparing tables and charts and Marie-Jeanette Ng Choy Hing, Françoise Stravel-Postic, and Nadine Dubost for providing very dependable secretarial support. Elisa Diehl of the IMF's External Relations Department edited the manuscript and coordinated production.

# I Overview

In January 1994, seven sub-Saharan African countries—Benin, Burkina Faso, Côte d'Ivoire, Mali, Niger, Senegal, and Togo—signed a treaty establishing the West African Economic and Monetary Union (WAEMU). These countries, with the addition of Guinea-Bissau in 1997, form part of the CFA franc zone along with a second group of six African countries that participate in a similar monetary arrangement, the Central African Economic and Monetary Community (CAEMC). The CAEMC countries are Cameroon, the Central African Republic, Chad, Republic of Congo, Equatorial Guinea, and Gabon. Within each subzone, monetary arrangements are managed by a separate central bank: the Central Bank of West African States (BCEAO) for the WAEMU and the Bank of Central African States (BEAC) for the CAEMC. The two subzones share a common currency, the CFA franc, which stands for the Communauté financière africaine in the BCEAO area and for the Coopération financière en Afrique in the BEAC area.

Member countries of each subzone agree to pool a minimum proportion of their gross foreign exchange reserves (currently 65 percent) in an operations account with the French treasury. Through this account, the French treasury provides an unlimited overdraft facility, thus guaranteeing the convertibility of the CFA franc. Since its introduction in 1948, the CFA franc has been pegged to the French franc, and, except for a devaluation in 1994, its parity has remained unchanged. Since January 12, 1994, the exchange rate has been fixed at CFAF 100 = F 1, compared with CFAF 50 = F 1 before the devaluation.

During the second half of the 1980s and in the early 1990s, a prolonged worsening of the terms of trade and a steep rise in labor costs, combined with a nominal appreciation of the French franc against the U.S. dollar, led to a considerable real effective appreciation of the CFA franc and a serious deterioration in the region's competitive position. As part of a comprehensive strategy to address this problem, the 14 countries of the CFA franc zone devalued their common currency by 50 percent in January 1994 and ceased to rely exclusively on measures of internal adjustment.

The exchange rate realignment led to a significant turnaround in economic activity in the CFA franc zone, and in the WAEMU in particular, with output, exports, and investment increasing rapidly during 1994–97. Inflation, after a brief surge in the aftermath of the devaluation, has returned to low levels. On the basis of a number of real exchange rate indicators, the competitive position of the WAEMU at this time appears to be broadly adequate, although the evolution of these indicators will need to be kept under close review.

## Policy Issues Facing the WAEMU

Despite these recent improvements, the WAEMU countries continue to grapple with a number of policy issues. First, the level of liquidity in the banking system is high, which appears to be related to various structural problems, including insufficient competition among banks, the limited role of the interbank market, administrative obstacles to cross-country banking activities, and the high risks associated with reimbursements of bank loans. Although the governments of the member countries have been actively involved in the restructuring efforts of a number of banks, they must now pursue full privatization to improve banks' efficiency and strengthen their financial structure. They should, in addition, revise capital adequacy ratios to make them consistent with international standards.

Second, in the area of trade policy, the WAEMU countries are planning to implement a common external tariff during 1998–2000, which will provide an opportunity to eliminate all tariff and nontariff barriers within the WAEMU, further liberalize external trade, and deepen the countries' integration with the world economy. Specifically, all tariffs on trade related to products that meet local content requirements will be eliminated among member countries, and the tariff structure that applies to trade with countries outside the WAEMU will be simplified.

A third major issue for the countries in the region will be to create the conditions for an increase in domestic and foreign private investment, which, despite some improvement in recent years, remain low. Necessary steps include streamlining the regulatory framework and eliminating the discriminatory practices and distortions associated with exemptions from customs duties and other taxes. The planned adoption of a regional investment code and the liberalization of trade that is expected to result from the implementation of the common external tariff should help them achieve this objective.

Finally, the WAEMU countries are seeking to fully harmonize business laws among themselves. The vehicle for this strategy is the Treaty on the Harmonization of Business Laws in Africa, adopted in October 1993. While it represents a major step in the right direction, the countries will need to follow it up by overhauling the judicial system.

## Institutional Framework of the WAEMU

The treaty establishing the WAEMU was signed on January 10, 1994 and entered into force on August 1, 1994 after its ratification by all member countries (see Box 1).[1] The aim of the treaty was to build on the achievements of the West African Monetary Union (WAMU), created in 1962, whose main objective was to provide the macroeconomic stability and the credibility required to sustain the fixed exchange rate for the common currency. The WAEMU treaty aims to extend the process of integration already at work in the monetary area to the whole economic sphere.[2] This goal will involve cre-

---

[1]Appendix I describes some of the main features of the WAEMU as a regional grouping and compares them with features of the European Union.

[2]At present, the WAEMU treaty coexists with the earlier WAMU treaty, but is expected eventually to replace it.

---

**Box 1. WAEMU: Institutional Framework**

The highest organ of the WAEMU is the Conference of the Heads of States and Governments. It meets at least once a year, determines the broad policy orientations of the WAEMU, and has authority for introducing new provisions into the treaty.

The Council of Ministers, which meets four times a year, is responsible for implementing the broad decisions of the Conference of the Heads of States and Governments. It decides on the adoption of the regional Banking Commission's proposals. The commission, responsible for bank supervision, makes recommendations on all policy issues relevant to the WAEMU other than those within the purview of the central bank, and implements the decisions of the Council of Ministers.

The acts of the Council of Ministers and of the regional Banking Commission are translated into rulings, instructions, or decisions that are mandatory for all parties concerned. The West African Development Bank, headquartered in Lomé, Togo, also plays an active supporting role in the economic integration effort of the WAEMU. Other regional institutions include The Court of Justice, the Consular Chamber of Commerce, and the Interparliamentary Committee.

---

ation of a single domestic market through the establishment of a customs union, harmonization of legal systems, implementation of common sectoral policies, and convergence of fiscal policies in support of the common monetary policy. The treaty provides a framework within which member countries can address a number of structural weaknesses that have limited their growth potential; strengthen the credibility and effectiveness of their economic policies; and achieve a number of benefits, including economies of scale and efficiency gains.

# II  Recent Economic Developments

During the second half of the 1980s and in the early 1990s, a prolonged deterioration of the terms of trade, a steep increase in labor costs, and the nominal appreciation of the French franc against the U.S. dollar resulted in a considerable real effective appreciation of the CFA franc (Figures 1 and 2 and Appendix II).[3] These developments led to a serious decline in the competitive position of the CFA franc zone and a substantial weakening of the economic situation in the region. For the WAEMU as a whole during 1990–93, real GDP growth per capita was negative, and savings and investment ratios were very low (see Table 1 and Appendix IV, Tables 4–13). The deterioration in the terms of trade, together with the slow growth of export volume, resulted in a widening of the external current account deficit to an average of 11 percent of GDP in 1990–93. The shrinking of the tax base caused by the decline in real income as well as the financial difficulties of most corporate taxpayers were reflected in a drop in the ratio of government revenue to GDP, a deterioration in the overall fiscal balance, and severe constraints on government investment. Consequently, there was a significant accumulation of both domestic and external payments arrears, a large increase in the public debt, and a decline in the net foreign assets of the BCEAO.

The 50 percent devaluation of the CFA franc in January 1994 was part of a comprehensive strategy through which the countries of the CFA franc zone

---

[3]This conclusion is based on the behavior of the internal real exchange rate, a proxy for the ratio of nontradable to tradable goods prices (Figure 1). For reasons explained in Appendix II, this concept of the real exchange rate is more relevant for small open economies than the one based on relative consumer prices.

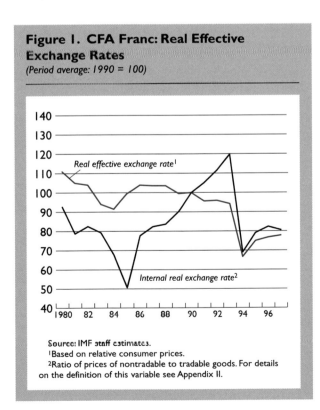

**Figure 1. CFA Franc: Real Effective Exchange Rates**
*(Period average: 1990 = 100)*

Source: IMF staff estimates.
[1]Based on relative consumer prices.
[2]Ratio of prices of nontradable to tradable goods. For details on the definition of this variable see Appendix II.

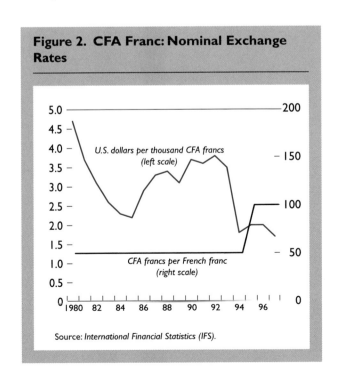

**Figure 2. CFA Franc: Nominal Exchange Rates**

Source: *International Financial Statistics (IFS)*.

## Table 1.  WAEMU:  Selected Economic Indicators

| | 1990–93 | 1994 | 1995 | 1996 | Prel. 1997 |
|---|---|---|---|---|---|
| | *(Annual percentage change)* | | | | |
| Real GDP growth | 0.2 | 3.2 | 5.7 | 6.0 | 5.6 |
| Real per capita GDP growth | −3.0 | −0.2 | 2.5 | 2.6 | 2.3 |
| Export volume | 3.6 | 8.8 | 8.6 | 13.0 | 8.8 |
| Import volume | −1.1 | −12.0 | 28.2 | 5.0 | 4.8 |
| Terms of trade | −1.9 | 2.0 | 4.3 | −3.1 | −3.9 |
| Inflation | 0.6 | 29.2 | 12.2 | 3.9 | 3.8 |
| | *(Percent of GDP)* | | | | |
| Overall fiscal balance[1] | −9.1 | −8.7 | −6.0 | −4.3 | −4.3 |
| Primary fiscal balance[1,2] | −3.9 | −3.4 | −1.2 | −0.2 | −0.7 |
| Government revenue[1] | 16.4 | 15.2 | 17.0 | 17.4 | 17.4 |
| External current account | −11.2 | −7.2 | −9.1 | −8.2 | −7.6 |
| Gross domestic savings | 7.3 | 13.6 | 13.5 | 14.6 | 15.7 |
| Gross domestic investment | 12.1 | 14.8 | 16.2 | 16.9 | 18.1 |
| Gross foreign assets, BCEAO[3] | 1.1 | 2.7 | 3.7 | 3.7 | 3.9 |
| Public external debt (end of period) | 85 | 132 | 113 | 109 | 103 |

Note: Excluding Guinea-Bissau.
[1]Excluding grants.
[2]Overall balance, excluding interest payments.
[3]In billions of U.S. dollars.

sought to address the problems just mentioned.[4] It was followed by a significant turnaround in the economies of most countries in the CFA franc zone and in the WAEMU in particular. The improved competitive position of the WAEMU resulted in sharp increases in the volume of exports after 1994, reflecting primarily the response of the traditional export sector to higher producer prices (Appendix, IV, Table 14). Import volumes fell sharply in 1994, reflecting import substitution in favor of agricultural and locally manufactured goods, which also contributed to a narrowing of the regional current account deficit. However, imports picked up strongly thereafter, owing to the rapid growth of real aggregate demand.

Improved profitability in the tradable goods sector, including nontraditional exports and import substitutes, led to stronger growth performance after 1994, which, together with an improvement in the aggregate financial position of governments in the region (see Appendix IV, Table 15), resulted in a large increase in the domestic saving ratio.[5] Invest-

ment also rose substantially in relation to GDP, owing mainly to a rise in the *private* investment ratio. However, both total and private investment ratios remain low by the standards of all developing countries and also in comparison with other sub-Saharan African countries (Table 2).

Following the surge in domestic prices associated with the devaluation, inflation declined rapidly to an average of just under 4 percent in 1996–97, reflecting the prudent fiscal and monetary policies followed by governments and the BCEAO, respectively (Table 1). The return of confidence in price stability and the improvement in the region's external current account were reflected in a large buildup in the BCEAO's gross foreign assets, from the equivalent of 19 percent of base money in 1993 to 95 percent in 1994 (five months of imports of goods and nonfactor services). During the same period, the balance of the operations account maintained with the French treasury improved from US$0.3 billion to US$1.7 billion. Finally, the external debt of WAEMU countries has dropped substantially since 1994, even though it remains high in most member countries.

Data for 1997 confirm the continued favorable economic performance of WAEMU member countries. For the region as a whole, growth is estimated at 5½ percent and inflation has subsided to less than 4 percent, saving and investment ratios have contin-

---

[4]For a more detailed discussion of the background of the 1994 devaluation, see Jean A.P. Clément and others, *Aftermath of the CFA Franc Devaluation,* IMF Occasional Paper No. 138 (Washington: International Monetary Fund, 1996).

[5]Historical relationships suggest that changes in government savings in sub-Saharan Africa tend to be offset only in part by opposite changes in private savings.

**Table 2. International Comparisons: Selected Indicators**

| | WAEMU | | Sub-Saharan Africa | | All Developing Countries | |
|---|---|---|---|---|---|---|
| | 1990–93 | 1994–97 | 1990–93 | 1994–97 | 1990–93 | 1994–97 |
| | *(Annual percentage change)* | | | | | |
| Real GDP | 0.2 | 5.0 | 1.6 | 3.7 | 5.5 | 6.3 |
| Real GDP per capita | –3.0 | 1.8 | –2.3 | 0.8 | 3.4 | 4.3 |
| Inflation[1] | 1.0 | 3.8 | 30.0 | 34.6 | 46.6 | 9.0 |
| | *(Percent of GDP)* | | | | | |
| Investment | 13.0 | 16.2 | 17.2 | 17.6 | 26.5 | 28.6 |
| Private investment | 7.7 | 10.1 | 12.3 | 12.2 | 15.8 | 16.6 |
| External current account [2] | –11.2 | –8.0 | –4.5 | –4.6 | –2.3 | –1.8 |

[1]Last year of the period; consumer prices (annual averages).
[2]Excluding grants.

ued to rise, and the overall fiscal position has remained stable. In the area of monetary policy, a strong pickup in credit demand was partially offset by a decline in BCEAO credit to governments, and gross foreign assets increased further, to the equivalent of 130 percent of base money. In spite of a deterioration in the terms of trade in 1996–97, the region's external current account deficit declined further as export volumes—including for nontraditional exports—continued to expand rapidly.

# III Main Regional Policy Issues

## Monetary Policy

The BCEAO conducts monetary policy in the WAEMU at the regional level. Its basic near-term objectives are (1) to maintain the fixed exchange rate relationship between the CFA franc and the French franc—which means that the trend rate of inflation in the area is fundamentally determined by French inflation (Box 2); and (2) to achieve a target level of foreign assets for the BCEAO. The fixed exchange rate system implies that the independence of *regional* monetary policy is constrained: money growth within the region is endogenously determined, and an appropriate differential must be maintained between market interest rates in the WAEMU and in France (Figure 3). Moreover, there is no scope for *national* monetary policies in the member countries of the WAEMU. For this reason, IMF-supported programs in these countries currently do not include targets for either base money or the central banks' net domestic assets because these variables cannot be meaningfully defined at the national level. Even if they could be defined, they would be beyond the control of the national authorities. Of course, fiscal policy—including public debt management—remains within the purview of individual countries in the WAEMU, and IMF-supported programs typically include targets for the fiscal deficit, external borrowing by the government, and net domestic bank credit to the government. Cumulative borrowing by national governments from the BCEAO is itself constrained to no more than 20 percent of their fiscal revenue in the previous year.

The BCEAO seeks to control domestic credit expansion in the region by using indirect monetary policy instruments and enforcing ceilings on central bank credit to governments. The policy instruments available to the BCEAO are the discount rate mechanism, a repurchase agreement facility (pension window), and a system of periodic auctions of central bank bills, as well as reverse auctions, introduced in July 1996.[6] Auctions and repurchase agreements are the most frequently used instruments; the discount rate is used primarily to signal policy intentions about future movements in interest rates. Ceilings on central bank credit to governments, set at the equivalent of 20 percent of tax revenue in the preceding year and generally observed by member countries, are a powerful tool of credit policy. However, they lack flexibility because the central bank cannot change them to accommodate its near-term policy objectives.

The goal of the regional monetary program for 1998, adopted by the BCEAO last December, is to strengthen the gross foreign assets of the central bank while allowing credit to the economy to expand in line with the projected rate of growth of nominal GDP. The net foreign assets of the BCEAO are targeted to grow by nearly 10 percent during 1998 over the previous year, which should allow for continued adequate coverage of the monetary base. In line with the objectives determined in each country of the WAEMU in the context of IMF-supported programs, net bank credit to WAEMU governments is expected to decline moderately.

A source of concern for both the monetary authorities and IMF staff in recent years has been the vast pool of unused liquid resources in the banking system (see Appendix IV, Tables 16–18). These resources consist of a large stock of unremunerated excess reserves at the central bank and sizable holdings of long-term government bonds consolidated by the WAEMU and short-term BCEAO bills.[7] At the end of 1996, the amount of liquid resources held by banks in these various forms amounted to almost 20 percent of bank deposits (Appendix IV, Table 18). This liquidity "overhang" tended to increase from 1994 to 1996, owing to the return of flight capital and the rise in export earnings that had to be repatriated and surrendered to the central bank, while the expansion of bank credit tended

---

[6]A system of reserve requirements has been in place since late 1993. However, the required reserve ratio is very low (1.5 percent of deposits) and has remained unchanged since 1993.

[7]The long-term consolidated bonds were issued by the BCEAO in 1994, in counterpart of its claims on member governments resulting from the restructuring of the banking system; they are de facto highly liquid because they can be redeemed on demand with the BCEAO. The short-term BCEAO bills are purchased through the periodic auction system introduced in 1996.

---

### Box 2. The CFA Franc, the French Franc, and the Euro

The parity between the CFA franc and the single European currency will be based automatically on the exchange rate between the French franc and the euro.[1] More specifically, the communiqué issued at the conclusion of the meeting of finance ministers of France and of the countries of the CFA franc zone, held in Libreville on April 10, 1998, indicates that

- the French franc will become a national denomination of the euro on January 1, 1999 at a parity that will be irrevocably fixed on that day and that it will be replaced by the euro on January 1, 2002;
- the cooperation agreements linking France and the two monetary unions within the CFA franc zone will be maintained and that France will continue to guarantee the convertibility of the CFA franc;
- the value of the euro in terms of the French franc will automatically determine the value of the CFA franc against the euro beginning January 1, 1999; and
- the move to the euro will have no implications for the denomination of transactions and settlements outside the euro zone; claims denominated in the currencies participating in the euro can be denominated either in those currencies or in euros beginning January 1, 1999, and will be denominated in euros beginning January 1, 2002.

---

[1]For a discussion of some of the issues involved, see Michael Hadjimichael and Michel Galy, "The CFA Franc Zone and the EMU," IMF Working Paper 97/156 (Washington: International Monetary Fund, 1997).

---

to lag behind the growth of nominal GDP. Credit expansion picked up strongly during 1997, and the ratio of liquid assets to deposits fell sharply, although it remained high at almost 17 percent.

The liquidity overhang seems to be related to a number of factors: (1) the high risk of bank loans to banks resulting from legal difficulties in enforcing the recovery of claims in case of default; (2) significant inefficiencies in the banking system at the regional level, which hinder the channeling of funds from very liquid banks in some member countries to banks in other countries where the demand for credit is relatively strong;[8] (3) a lack of competition among banks, particularly at the regional level; and (4) the weakness of credit demand from a number of large borrowers, in particular in the export-oriented sector,

who experienced substantial improvements in their cash flow and improved access to external credit after the 1994 devaluation.

The first three factors—high lending risk, lack of competition, and other financial market imperfections—appear to be consistent with the simultaneous occurrence until recently of excess liquidity and slow credit expansion and also with the existence of high spreads between deposit and loan rates in the region. The fourth explanation, which features the strong cash-flow position of export-oriented companies, could help to explain weak demand for bank credit in recent years. While not a cause of immediate concern in view of the sluggishness of credit expansion in the past several years, the recent surge in bank credit suggests that the central bank must stand ready to absorb any excess liquidity in the system if and when the need arises—for example, if strong demand for credit coincides with the resolution of some of the structural problems noted above. If the use of reserve requirements or auctions of central bank bills prove insufficient, additional measures—including the issuance of central bank medium-term bonds (not redeemable on demand) carrying a suitable rate of interest—might also be considered. While not ruling out this possibility, the BCEAO feels that the need for such bonds is not required in present circumstances in view of the prudence of the banks' lending policies.

## Banking System

As indicated above, some of the key monetary policy issues in the WAEMU are closely related to a number of structural problems of the region's banking system, which need to be addressed both to increase efficiency in financial intermediation and to improve monetary control. First, competition among banks in the WAEMU appears to be insufficient in at least two ways: (1) lending rates, except for preferred customers, remain high in real terms; and (2) the lack of competition for depositors is evidenced by low deposit rates and occasional refusals by banks to accept term deposits by customers. The lack of competition is illustrated by a large gap between the costs of funds to banks and their lending rates and, therefore, by a high level of profitability of most banks in the region.[9]

Because they are so profitable at present, the banks lack incentives to modify their strategy and develop more aggressive lending policies. In addition, the unreliability of the judicial system and, in some countries, the apparent bias of legal procedures

---

[8]Banks in Senegal and Côte d'Ivoire tend to be less liquid than those in other WAEMU countries. However, Senegalese and Ivoirien banks are usually refinanced through the central bank rather than through the regional interbank market.

[9]The average cost of resources in the WAEMU is about 2 percent, while lending rates range from 6 percent to 15 percent.

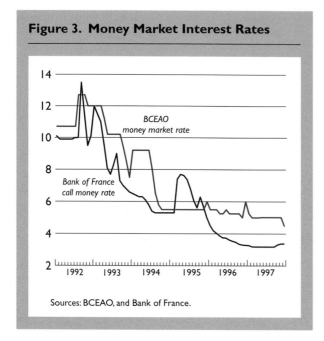

**Figure 3. Money Market Interest Rates**

BCEAO
money market rate

Bank of France
call money rate

Sources: BCEAO, and Bank of France.

in favor of debtors represent serious obstacles to the recovery of claims and encourage some borrowers to default on their loans. Thus, the risk to banks that would result from a more aggressive lending policy should not be underestimated. However, the rapid development of small mutual savings and lending institutions during the last five years in both urban and rural areas shows that it is possible for financial institutions to lend actively while experiencing only very limited rates of nonperforming credits.

One way to improve the functioning of the region's banking system would be for the BCEAO to encourage the development of an active interbank market. Indications about volume, interest spreads, and accessibility suggest that the interbank market is working imperfectly; only a few of the approximately fifty banks operating in the WAEMU participate actively in the market. Insufficient information about the financial strength of participants and the absence of an efficient payment system also hamper the functioning of the interbank market. As a first step toward improving the flow of information, the BCEAO has started to provide market participants with data on interbank loans, including the volume of transactions and the weighted average rate. In addition, a reform of the payment system is currently under way and should promote the development of interbank transactions. The efficiency and competitiveness of the banking system could also be improved through the introduction of a single, zone-wide licensing agreement for banks in the WAEMU. Currently, banks are required to have a banking license and a separate capital base in each country in

which they wish to operate, discouraging them from operating across borders. While supportive of a zone-wide licensing agreement, the BCEAO faces resistance from WAEMU governments, which fear that an increase in the number of banks operating in their respective countries could increase their liability in the event of bank failure.

## Bank Supervision

The financial sector of the WAEMU includes 53 banks and 26 financial institutions (Appendix IV, Table 19). At most, 10 of the 53 banks are considered large—with assets of more than CFAF 100 billion (US$170 million)—and offer a wide variety of services to a broad range of customers throughout the region. The financial situation of the banking system has improved significantly in most WAEMU countries since the early 1990s as a result of restructuring operations that have raised banks' equity base and retained profits. Net profits for 1996 amounted to about CFAF 73 billion (US$140 million), compared with CFAF 12 billion (US$22 million) in 1994, and were equivalent to 25 percent of capital for all banks taken as a group (and to 35 percent of capital for the 10 largest banks). The number of banks unable to observe the minimum capital requirement ratio fell from 17 in 1994 to 13 in 1996; of these 13 banks, all except 1 were small or medium-sized. The share of nonperforming loans declined from 32 percent in 1993 to less than 20 percent in 1996.

Responsibility for bank supervision rests primarily with the regional Banking Commission, established in 1990. However, the ministries of finance of individual member countries and the BCEAO retain final authority, and their agreement is necessary for the most important decisions involving commercial banks and other financial institutions, including closure in the interest of depositors. By and large, the Banking Commission has supervised the banking system effectively. With the recent strengthening of its personnel, it has been able to inspect about half of the banks operating in the WAEMU and to carry out more frequent partial controls over banks on its "close watch" list—about one-fourth of active banks. The quality of the inspections it performs and of the reports it produces is generally considered to be high. However, in many cases, the recommendations of the Banking Commission tend to be implemented with long delays, especially when the issue is strengthening the capital base of banks considered to be financially unsound.

Governments have been actively involved in the restructuring efforts of a number of banks in financial difficulty—an involvement that is unavoidable when the banks are entirely or partly owned by the state. The political pressure to ensure full repayment of deposits when banks fail and depositors lose money explains, to a large extent, the reluctance of most governments to accept the closure of banks as a solution. Governments should seek full privatization of the banking system, which would diminish this pressure. The need to raise capital ratios to international standards should also receive prompt attention. The capital adequacy ratio currently in place in the WAEMU (4 percent) does not accurately reflect the level of risk faced by banks operating in the region, and a minimum ratio of 8 percent should be considered.

## Trade Policy

The WAEMU treaty provides for the elimination of all tariff and nontariff barriers between member countries as well as for the rationalization and harmonization of trade policies vis-à-vis third countries through the elimination of nontariff barriers and the implementation of a common external tariff. Despite efforts to liberalize trade in recent years, and especially since the 1994 devaluation, import duties are generally still high in the WAEMU, especially in Burkina Faso, Côte d'Ivoire, and Senegal. These high tariffs have usually been justified on the basis of the narrowness of the tax base, but they have also served in many instances to protect local industries. The move to a common external tariff thus provides an opportunity for member countries to harmonize and rationalize their individual tariff structures, further liberalize external trade, and deepen their integration with the world economy.

In its dialogue with both the national authorities and the regional Banking Commission, the IMF staff has argued that the common external tariff should involve a reduction in tariff peaks, a simplification of the tariff schedule, and a reduction in the average external duty rate to the lowest level consistent with reducing fiscal imbalances. In line with the principles of the World Trade Organization, the staff has also cautioned against the adoption of a tariff structure that would raise the tariffs in those member countries with the lowest rates, such as Benin and Togo. In view of the relatively small economic size of the WAEMU and the relatively low level of trade among its members (see Appendix I), it should be possible to reduce intraregional levels of protection substantially while liberalizing trade with the rest of the world, resulting in considerable trade creation with very little trade diversion.

On November 28, 1997, the Council of Ministers adopted a precise calendar for introducing the common external tariff. The ultimate objective is to put in place by January 1, 2000, a structure that consists of four rates: 0, 5, 10, and 20 percent (see Box 3). In the first phase of the transition (from July 1, 1998 to December 31, 1998), all import duties will be subject to an overall ceiling of 30 percent. In the second phase, starting January 1, 1999, the number of rates will be limited to four: 0, 5, 10, and a temporary maximum rate of 25 percent. On top of the tariff rates that will be in place by January 2000, there will be a statistical tax not to exceed 1 percent that, for some countries, will represent a sharp reduction from existing levels. In addition, a few products—still to be identified—could be subject to import surtaxes on a transitory basis. Safeguard measures, however, may be applied in specific circumstances to protect local industries or producers from erratic fluctuations in international prices.

With regard to the liberalization of trade within the WAEMU, the 60 percent preference margin relative to the tariff rate applicable to countries outside the union in July 1997 will be raised to 80 percent in January 1999 and to 100 percent in January 2000. These steps will eliminate by the latter date all internal tariffs on trade between member countries related to *eligible* industrial products—that is, those with a regional value added equal to at least 40 percent of total value added or with a regional content of at least 60 percent. All duties on agricultural products and handicrafts were eliminated in July 1996.

The common tariff structure to be put in place over the next two years will need to be based on a detailed classification of imports to be adopted by July 1, 1998.[10] In discussions with WAEMU representatives and national authorities, the IMF staff noted that the categorization of products that was under consideration was biased toward the protection of local industries in that it allowed products identified as "sensitive" to be shifted into categories that afforded the maximum allowable tariff rate. Accordingly, the staff recommended, with support from the World Bank, the adoption of a categorization of goods similar to the one established by the United Nations, which is strictly based on the level of processing of the goods (that is, primary, capital, and consumption goods). The staff also argued that the use of any exceptional surtax should be temporary and truly exceptional (that is, limited to a very small number of tariff lines).

The lower duties implied by the common external tariff could substantially reduce fiscal revenue in a

---

[10]The broad classification of products envisaged by the WAEMU Commission in November 1997 is as follows: category I: essential goods (for example, medical supplies and school books); category II: raw materials and capital goods; category III: intermediate goods; category IV: final consumption goods. The revised classification is expected to be finalized by the end of June 1998.

### Box 3.  WAEMU:  New Tariff Structure

| | From July 1, 1998 | From January 1, 1999 | From January 1, 2000 |
|---|---|---|---|
| **External tariff** | | | |
| Category   I | Current rate | 0 | 0 |
| Category   II | Current rate | Maximum 5% | 5% |
| Category   III | Current rate | Maximum 10% | 10% |
| Category   IV | Maximum 30% | Maximum 25% | 20% |
| Regional tax[1] | 0.5% | 0.5% | 0.5% |
| Statistical tax | Current rate[2] or less | Current rate[2] or less | Maximum 1% |
| **Intra-WAEMU tariff** | | | |
| Local agricultural products | 0 | 0 | 0 |
| Approved industrial products of origin[3] | 60% preference[4] | 80% preference[4] | 100% preference |
| Nonapproved industrial products of origin | −5 percentage points | −5 percentage points | ... |
| Other products | No preference | No preference | ... |

[1]Levied on all imported goods to assist in meeting the budgetary cost of regional institutions and to finance structural regional funds and the revenue shortfall resulting from the regional preference margin.

[2]Rates currently vary from 1 percent to 6 percent.

[3]Products with a minimum local content of 40 percent.

[4]Over external tariff rate.

number of WAEMU countries where import duty rates are currently high. Several of the countries that are most likely to be affected have requested technical assistance from the IMF to quantify the potential impact of the common external tariff and help them find ways to offset the expected losses. A recent IMF technical assistance mission to Burkina Faso estimated the revenue loss associated with the introduction of the common external tariff at 0.9 percent of GDP by the year 2000. This estimate assumes the implementation of certain compensatory fiscal measures, including an increase in excise taxes on petroleum products. A similar study for Senegal has shown that the fiscal cost, exclusive of compensatory measures, would be equivalent to 1 percent of GDP during 1998–99 and 1.6 percent in 2000. Simulations performed by the customs administration in Côte d'Ivoire indicate that revenue shortfalls would be very limited in that country, provided that exemptions are virtually eliminated. In discussions with both regional and national authorities, the IMF staff has stressed that countries must offset revenue losses as much as possible by introducing compensatory revenue measures and, in particular, by eliminating exemptions on import duties and other taxes. At the same time, the staff has indicated that, if countries make such efforts, and if they are implementing an otherwise strong reform program, the IMF would take into consideration any temporary, residual ef-

fect of tariff reduction on fiscal revenue in identifying the financing of the program.

In parallel with adopting the common external tariff, WAEMU members are working together to harmonize indirect taxation. In this regard, the regional Banking Commission is developing proposals for a value-added tax, excises, and a tax on petroleum products, for which the IMF is providing technical assistance. In December 1997, the Council of Ministers considered a general framework for harmonizing indirect taxation and will address recommendations to member countries before the end of 1998, with the objective of achieving effective harmonization by 2000.

## Coordination of Macroeconomic Policies

The WAEMU treaty aims at convergence of economic policies and performance among member countries through a mechanism of multilateral surveillance. The WAMU treaty had already specified a number of common rules in the monetary area, in particular on central bank credit to governments, the minimum level of official foreign assets, and the legal framework under which commercial banks operate. Convergence is expected to be achieved through

---

### Box 4. WAEMU: Convergence Criteria

Article 4b of the WAEMU treaty establishes the principle of a gradual convergence of economic performance of member countries. Accordingly, convergence criteria to facilitate monitoring of progress in the context of the multilateral surveillance on economic performance have been developed in the area of public finance. The common objectives set by these criteria are as follows:

- A level of civil service wage bill not to exceed 50 percent of tax revenue (lowered to 40 percent from January 1998).
- A level of public investment financed by domestic resources equal to at least 20 percent of tax revenue.
- A primary basic fiscal surplus equivalent to at least 15 percent of tax revenue.
- A declining or unchanged level of domestic arrears.
- A declining or unchanged level of external arrears.

For 1997, the performance of member countries in terms of these convergence criteria was estimated as follows by the regional commission:

| | Wage Bill | Investment Financed by Domestic Resources | Basic Primary Balance | Change in Domestic Arrears | Change in External Arrears |
|---|---|---|---|---|---|
| | *(Percent of tax revenue)* | | | *(Billions of CFA francs)* | |
| Benin | 38 | 7 | 21 | −17 | — |
| Burkina Faso | 40 | 23 | 9 | −6 | — |
| Côte d'Ivoire | 37 | 22 | 24 | −52 | — |
| Mali | 30 | 18 | 27 | −7 | — |
| Niger | 57 | 7 | −8 | −21 | 2 |
| Senegal | 40 | 14 | 29 | — | 3 |
| Togo | 51 | 3 | 6 | −23 | −17 |

- basic rules and quantitative criteria related to some key policy areas, such as fiscal policies, incomes policies, and external debt management;
- harmonized statistical indicators to monitor the observance of adopted norms;
- periodic reviews by the regional Banking Commission of the performance of individual countries; and
- in cases of serious divergence, a process involving consultation and coordination, and, at some point, disciplinary actions against individual countries failing to implement corrective measures. So far, however, this process remains untested.

Five indicators are used to monitor the convergence of fiscal policies in the WAEMU area, all of them defined in relation to tax revenue (see Box 4 and Appendix IV, Table 20). Member countries are also expected to gradually eliminate all domestic and external payments arrears. Indicators of economic performance for 1997 suggest that all member countries except Burkina Faso, Niger, and Togo met the convergence criterion on the basic primary balance.[11] Only Burkina Faso and Côte d'Ivoire observed the criterion on domestically financed investment, while Mali is within reach of the 20 percent threshold. All countries have satisfied the criterion on the wage bill except Burkina Faso, Niger, and Togo, which are close to the target. All member countries except Niger have eliminated external payments arrears, and Benin, Burkina Faso, and Senegal have eliminated domestic payments arrears. The recent adoption by the Council of Ministers of two decisions designed to harmonize budget laws and government accounts in the WAEMU as a whole by 2000 is expected to further strengthen the basis for multilateral surveillance. IMF technical assistance in the area of fiscal convergence has been requested and is being considered.

---

[11]Defined as total revenue minus expenditure and net lending, excluding interest payments and externally financed capital expenditure.

# IV Other Regional Issues

As a key element in the achievement of sustainable long-run growth, investment is given top priority in the development of the WAEMU's economic policy. On average, rates of investment in the WAEMU are comparatively low.[12] A major objective of the regional investment code in preparation, which is intended to replace all existing codes in member countries, is to promote investment through simpler and more transparent rules. It also seeks to correct discriminatory practices that are based on the type of economic activity, the nationality of the beneficiaries, and the size of the relevant enterprises. Another objective is to avoid the distortions associated with exemptions from customs duties and other indirect taxes. In the view of the IMF staff, however, the project as it now stands does not go far enough in the direction of eliminating exemptions, notably those on customs duties on equipment and investment goods as well as those on the value-added tax on imports and local goods and services.

To promote the development of the private sector, WAEMU countries have decided to create a privately owned regional securities exchange, which is expected to become operational in mid-1998. Given its wide regional base, the securities exchange should increase the number of companies currently listed on the national stock exchange operating in Abidjan. It should also facilitate the implementation of WAEMU countries' privatization programs and help raise small investors' participation in the financing of enterprises. The necessary supervision of financial markets will be ensured by the Regional Securities and Exchange Council, created in 1996 by the WAEMU Council of Ministers. Its mandate includes not only supervising all activities of the exchange, but also regulating and authorizing all financial instruments issued by borrowers on the market.

The bias in favor of tax exemptions that still exists in the draft common investment code—which the IMF staff has urged the authorities to correct promptly—appears to represent a vicious circle inherent in the preferential regimes put in place over a number of years in all WAEMU countries. The narrowing of the tax base resulting from such preferential regimes leads to excessively high nominal rates of taxation—reducing people's incentives to produce and invest—and these high tax rates, in turn, provide a strong incentive for firms to seek tax exemptions. Thus, the staff has impressed on the WAEMU's regional and national authorities the need to move forcefully and simultaneously to cut exemptions and reduce import duties in the context of the common external tariff as complementary steps to improve incentives and raise the efficiency and the fairness of the tax system.

An important element of the strategy adopted by WAEMU member countries is to fully harmonize business laws through the Treaty on the Harmonization of Business Laws in Africa (OHADA), adopted in October 1993 by 15 African countries (all the CFA franc countries and Comoros). It is designed to unify business laws, promote arbitration procedures to resolve contractual conflicts, and improve the professional training of magistrates and their auxiliaries. It calls for a framework of rules to apply to all corporate and individual businesses, a set of rules for the use of guarantees and other forms of collateral in support of business transactions, procedures governing the resolution of bankruptcy proceedings and loan recovery, and accounting laws applicable to enterprises. WAEMU members have made progress toward achieving these objectives, notably with the establishment of a regional court of justice and arbitration in 1997 and the recent entry into force of three Uniform Acts, adopted in 1997 by the OHADA Council of Ministers. These acts, which do not require further approval and are directly enforceable in all member countries, go a long way in the direction of full harmonization of business laws in the WAEMU. They will soon be complemented by two additional acts, which were adopted by the Council of Ministers in April 1998. These acts establish simplified procedures for loan recovery and a framework for settling liabilities in cases of bankruptcy; they are expected to come into force on July 10,

---

[12]The results reported in Appendix III suggest that low investment ratios in the region reflect insufficient competition among businesses in domestic markets, excessive regulation, and a lack of openness to international trade and capital movements.

1998 and January 1, 1999, respectively. The recently created regional court of justice and arbitration can hear all cases related to the implementation of the Uniform Acts, and its decisions are enforceable in all the countries that have ratified the OHADA Treaty.

In parallel to the efforts made to harmonize business laws, the WAEMU authorities decided, in September 1996, to launch a regional project aimed at creating a common accounting framework for all nonfinancial businesses and corporations. The *Système comptable ouest africain,* which is expected to become fully operational by January 1, 1999, will ensure that all accounting systems used in the region generate information that is both reliable and capable of meeting the requirements and needs of all users.

Efforts to create a set of comparable economic indicators for countries in the WAEMU have already produced a harmonized index of consumer prices based on a common methodology. Other projects involve the harmonization of fiscal data, external and domestic debt, national accounts, and balance of payments. A uniform analytical framework for the public finances has been put in place, and progress is being made in compiling balance of payments and monetary statistics with technical assistance from the IMF. These are important steps that should now be followed by efforts to improve and harmonize national accounts data. To assist in the preparation of other key economic aggregates, WAEMU members, together with other member countries of the CFA franc zone, created a regional statistical office, which became operational in 1996. Its role is to advise and provide technical support to national statistical agencies in the preparation of aggregate data and to assist in conducting surveys and studies in key areas, such as the informal sector. With assistance from external donors, the office is currently lending support to member countries in institution building; harmonization of statistical nomenclatures; national accounting compilation methods; and studies on competitiveness, economic trends, and the contribution of informal businesses to overall economic activity.

The WAEMU treaty specifies a number of areas of common interest to its member countries. Specific sectoral policies need to be put in place in these areas to facilitate the achievement of the countries' macroeconomic policy objectives: human resource development, transport and telecommunications, environment, agriculture, energy, industry, and mining. Work on some of these areas (especially transport and communications) has recently begun in coordination with donors, notably the World Bank and the European Union, but it will take some time before concrete results can be achieved.

# V  Conclusions

Economic performance in the WAEMU has improved considerably since the devaluation of the CFA franc in 1994. The growth of output has increased rapidly and now exceeds population growth by a substantial margin, exports and investment have recovered strongly, and budgetary and external imbalances have narrowed. Moreover, after a brief surge in the aftermath of the devaluation, inflation has returned to low levels. However, while the ratio of investment to GDP has risen since 1994, it remains low by the standards of other developing countries and even in comparison with other countries of sub-Saharan Africa, thus raising some questions about the sustainability of strong growth.

The fixed exchange rate regime adopted by WAEMU countries has been operating without interruption since 1948, except for the single change in the exchange rate peg in January 1994. This degree of stability testifies to the prudence of the BCEAO's monetary policy during this period and to the ability of governments to pursue supportive fiscal policies. At the same time, the subordination of monetary policy to the objective of defending the fixed exchange rate and the level of international reserves has not been costless in terms of growth and employment. The overdue exchange rate realignment of 1994 has demonstrated the capacity of WAEMU countries to implement in a coordinated fashion a comprehensive set of measures geared toward reestablishing competitiveness and restoring confidence in their economies. At present, the IMF staff, on the basis of an examination of a number of exchange rate indicators and the behavior of the external current account, considers the competitive position of the WAEMU to be broadly adequate. In the future, the evolution of these indicators will need to be kept under close review.

The monetary policy pursued by the BCEAO has made an important contribution to macroeconomic stability in the region. A number of steps would help these countries improve efficiency in the financial sector in the future. The central bank should improve the functioning of the regional interbank market to allow banks to channel their excess reserves to less liquid banks elsewhere in the WAEMU, thus con-

tributing to the elimination of distortions and inefficiencies. The monetary authorities should also enhance competition between financial institutions. Lack of competition at present, particularly in view of the limited number of banks operating in the fragmented domestic markets, unduly raises lending rates and lowers the remuneration of deposits. The authorities should allow banks to open branches throughout the WAEMU and encourage them to compete for deposits and loans, which would improve the efficiency of the banking system and raise both private saving and investment. However, even if competition is improved, the supply of bank credit is likely to remain unduly constrained as long as the problems associated with loan recovery are not seriously addressed. Therefore, the IMF staff welcomes the efforts of the national authorities to improve the legal and judiciary environment. The entry into effect of the first Uniform Acts of OHADA will also contribute to this objective.

Another major preoccupation of the authorities is the need to further improve the soundness of the banking system. While they have made progress in the last few years, doubts remain about the financial situation of a number of institutions in need of restructuring. In particular, the rehabilitation plans for such banks should aim at a complete restoration of their equity base. In that context, the authorities should move to raise capital adequacy ratios to international standards.

The IMF staff believes that the success of WAEMU's common trade policy hinges on its ability to liberalize the region's trade regime. The common external tariff, to be phased in by January 1, 2000, represents an opportunity to achieve this goal. It should help raise productivity and incomes and improve the region's integration into the world economy by simplifying the present structure of import duties, lowering average tariff rates, and eliminating tariff peaks. However, it will be important for the WAEMU countries to avoid protectionist considerations in the final determination of the product classification scheme that they work out. Moreover, the application of any surtax should be severely limited in terms of level, coverage, and duration, and "statistical taxes" should be lowered in all countries as quickly as possible to the target level of 1 percent.

In the long run, the economic benefits resulting from the reallocation of resources and the improvement in competition made possible by the common external tariff should more than compensate for the losses that will unavoidably affect some producers in the region. In the near term, the reduction in average duties will have an adverse effect on government revenue in some countries. Although the decline in revenue should be compensated for through the reduction or elimination of exemptions on import duties and through other taxes, a transitional net revenue loss may well remain in a few countries. The resulting decline in government saving, if investment is to be protected, could lead to a transitory balance of payments gap. In those cases, and in the context of a strong program that includes strengthening the tax and customs administration, the possibility of additional, temporary financial support from the IMF and the World Bank will have to be considered.

A major challenge for the WAEMU will be to increase private investment, both domestic and foreign. The adoption of a common investment code should provide an opportunity to reduce or eliminate the tax incentives granted to domestic and foreign investors under existing regimes. In particular, the streamlining and harmonization of tax regimes under way in the WAEMU should allow governments to eliminate existing fiscal exemptions and preferences, which introduce serious distortions and deprive national treasuries of potentially large sources of revenue. A specific feature of the investment codes of WAEMU member countries is that they grant incentives in terms of value-added tax and tariff reductions, as well as corporate income tax incentives. The reduction or elimination in exemptions—under the value-added tax, in particular— would in many instances go a long way toward offsetting the revenue shortfalls resulting from lower tariffs. This reduction should go hand in hand with ambitious efforts to streamline the regulatory environment in which most enterprises function. In this respect, the harmonization of business laws represents a major achievement. The countries should take the next step of overhauling the functioning of the judicial system, which in many instances is an important source of significant delays and unreliable rulings.

# Appendix I  Comparison of Regional Integration: The WAEMU and the European Union

The two regions present an interesting contrast. Forty years after the Treaty of Rome, the European Union (EU) has created a customs union and achieved extensive regional economic and political integration, but is only now moving to a single currency. By contrast, the West African Economic and Monetary Union has had a single currency for 50 years, but a common external tariff is still in the planning stages, and other aspects of regional integration are far less developed than in Europe. The extent of reported intraregional trade (as a proportion of total trade of member countries) gives a striking, though somewhat exaggerated,[13] measure of the difference in trade integration between the two regions. Despite sharing a common currency, the countries of WAEMU trade little among themselves; most of their exports and imports are with industrial countries. In relation to total international trade, reported internal trade in the WAEMU is even significantly below that of the rest of Africa.

## Intraregional Exports
*(Percent of total exports)*

|                | 1993 | 1996 |
|----------------|------|------|
| European Union | 61.5 | 61.2 |
| WAEMU          | 8.4  | 9.1  |
| Other Africa   | 13.1 | 10.5 |

Source: IMF, *Direction of Trade Statistics* (Washington), various years.

The WAEMU and the EU differ considerably in their regional institutional and legal structures. In Europe, security as well as political considerations have reinforced the economic rationale for integration and have given rise to intergovernmental bodies with clear supranational authority in particular areas. The European Commission has executive responsibility in such areas as trade negotiations and competition policy, the European Court of Justice has its own areas of jurisdiction, and the European Parliament is directly elected. In addition, the European Council can make decisions through qualified majority voting, helping to avoid paralysis of decision making in areas for which the European institutions do not have supranational authority. In the WAEMU, supranationality to date has effectively been limited to the central bank for the region (the BCEAO) and to the regional Banking Commission.

Since the creation of the WAEMU in 1994, which broadened the scope of the existing WAMU, a more ambitious form of regional integration is being put in place that will include surveillance over member country policies through the monitoring of convergence criteria. The criteria (discussed in the body of the text) resemble the fiscal criteria of the EU (budget deficits and debt), but are focused more closely on the composition of government expenditures: wage bill, elimination of arrears, and primary surplus. Sanctions may be imposed on countries that do not observe the criteria, although details have not been worked out. In contrast, the countries proceeding to Economic and Monetary Union in the EU will be subject to the Stability and Growth Pact, which contains detailed procedures and considerable fines for those countries running excessive fiscal deficits. In the WAEMU, the danger of excessive deficits is reduced by the existence of ceilings on each member government's reliance on central bank financing. In effect, the fixed exchange rate link between the CFA franc and the French franc provides a tight constraint on money growth and budgetary profligacy.

In the European Union, the Treaty of Rome kicked off the integration process with a schedule for eliminating internal tariffs and quotas and moving to a common external tariff. These measures were accompanied by the management of agricultural production and important transfers to farmers in the context of the Common Agricultural Policy. By contrast, the WAEMU region has been slow to achieve a customs union. Tariffs were eliminated in 1996 on agricultural products, and preferential rates are applied on internally produced industrial goods. A common external tariff is scheduled to be phased in during 1998–2000.

---

[13]Informal trade is probably more significant for WAEMU countries, and other current account transactions, in particular workers' remittances, are substantial.

# Appendix II    The Real Exchange Rate of the WAEMU

This appendix calculates several indices of the real exchange rate for the WAEMU as a whole during 1970–97. The WAEMU economies maintain a fixed nominal exchange rate vis-à-vis the French franc, which remained unchanged from 1948 to January 1994, when the parity was devalued by 50 percent. The following questions are examined: To what extent had the real exchange rate appreciated before the devaluation of 1994? Was the nominal devaluation effective in improving competitiveness, and, if so, did the improvement last in the years following the devaluation?

There are two main definitions of the real exchange rate: the external real exchange rate and the internal real exchange rate. The *external real exchange rate* is the ratio of a domestic price or cost index to a weighted average of the corresponding index in foreign countries. The real exchange rate as measured by relative prices may not be appropriate for measuring competitiveness in small open economies because the price of tradable goods is determined in world markets. Domestic price changes therefore do not necessarily reflect changes in production costs. Moreover, trade barriers drive a wedge between foreign and domestic prices of tradable goods, so that changes in trade policy will change the external real exchange rate even though production costs do not change. It is therefore preferable to calculate the external real exchange rate as a ratio of production costs. The ratio of domestic to foreign wages or unit labor costs is often chosen because labor costs represent the largest proportion of total production costs.

The terms of trade have also been used as a measure of the external real exchange rate. This approach is based on the assumptions that the export price proxies the domestic deflator and that the import price proxies the foreign deflator. However, the first assumption is not expected to hold for small economies with undiversified exports, as is the case for the economies in the WAEMU that export primary products. In this case, the export price index is not representative of domestic prices because it measures the prices of only a few commodities. Furthermore, both the export and import price components of the terms of trade are determined in world markets, and changes of the nominal exchange rate therefore have no impact on them.

The *internal real exchange rate* is the ratio of the price of nontradable goods to the price of tradable goods. This measure relies only on domestic price indices and may therefore be more appropriate for small economies with relatively high trade barriers. The price of nontradables is influenced by their cost of production and may thus be more relevant as a measure of competitiveness.[14]

This appendix provides estimates of the external and internal real exchange rates for the WAEMU. The external real exchange rate is measured here as the ratio of domestic to foreign consumer price indices (CPI). Unfortunately, owing to unavailability of cost data for these economies, it was not possible to estimate a measure of relative costs. The internal real exchange rate, which has some of the advantages of a measure of relative costs, is calculated as the price ratio of nontradables to imports (the latter being a proxy for tradable goods).[15]

Both measures show that the real exchange rate depreciated sharply in 1994 and that it appreciated in the following three years, although a substantial margin of improvement remains relative to 1994. These results suggest that the devaluation of 1994, together with the accompanying policies, improved the competitive position of the region and that the competitiveness gains have been broadly maintained. The evolution of domestic costs and prices will nonetheless need to be carefully monitored to avoid a recurrence of the overvaluation of the early 1990s.

---

[14]For an extensive comparison of the external and the internal real exchange rate, see Lawrence E. Hinkle and Fabien Nsengiyumva, "The Relationship Between and Interpretation of External and Internal Real Exchange Rates: Competitiveness, Productivity, and the Terms of Trade," in *Estimating Equilibrium Exchange Rates in Developing Countries,* ed. by Lawrence E. Hinkle and Peter J. Montiel (unpublished; Washington: World Bank, 1997).

[15]Other measures were also calculated, but for various reasons the indices chosen seemed to be the most satisfactory.

The results are more mixed before 1994. On average, the external real exchange rate shows no appreciation of the real exchange rate before the devaluation of the nominal exchange rate in 1994. In contrast, the internal real exchange rate shows a significant appreciation before 1994, tending to confirm the theoretical presumption that the internal real exchange rate is a superior measure for these economies.

## Measuring the Real Exchange Rate

The external real exchange rate *(RERX)* is calculated here as the ratio of consumer price indices:

$$RERX = CPI_d / (CPI_f \bar{E}),$$

where $CPI_d$ and $CPI_f$ are the domestic and foreign consumer price indices, respectively, and $\bar{E}$ is the nominal exchange rate expressed in CFA francs per unit of foreign currency. An increase of the ratio implies an appreciation of the real exchange rate. Both $CPI_f$ and $\bar{E}$ are weighted averages for major trading partners, with bilateral trade shares used as the weights. *RERX* index is calculated for each of the seven economies of the WAEMU, and the national indices are then used to calculate a GDP-weighted average *RERX* for the WAEMU region (which is the one reported here). Box 5 shows the weights (GDP-weighted averages for the WAEMU) for the foreign price index in the calculations of the *RERX*.

The internal real exchange rate *(RERN)* is the ratio of nontradable to tradable goods prices. When the price of nontradable goods increases in relation to the price of tradable goods, factors of production move to the nontradables sector. To avoid such a reallocation of resources, a devaluation of the nominal exchange rate or a tightening of aggregate demand may be necessary. This is often the case when economic agents perceive as permanent a temporary resource "boom" in an economy that exports primary products.

The difficulty in measuring the internal real exchange rate is that there is no operationally straightforward definition of tradable and nontradable goods. As a result, the literature uses a variety of approximations.[16] In the measure calculated here, the price of imports $(P_m)$ is used for the price of tradable goods. An alternative would be to use the price of exports, but for economies with undiversified exports, the import price index is more representative of tradable goods prices.[17]

---

[16]See Lawrence E. Hinkle, and Fabien Nsengiyumva, "Internal Real Exchange Rates: Concepts and Measurement," in Hinkle and Montiel (1997).

[17]The results do not change significantly if the price of tradable goods is defined as the average of the indices of export and import prices.

---

| Box 5. Weights for Calculating the External Real Exchange Rate | | | |
|---|---|---|---|
| France | 28.23 | Netherlands | 5.82 |
| United States | 10.09 | United Kingdom | 5.50 |
| Germany | 9.95 | Belgium | 5.23 |
| Japan | 7.24 | Spain | 3.23 |
| Italy | 7.04 | Canada | 2.53 |

Source: IMF, *International Financial Statistics (IFS)* (Washington), various issues.

Note: GDP-weighted averages for the WAEMU, calculated on the basis of trade shares during 1988–91.

The price of nontradables $(P_n)$ is calculated on the basis of the domestic CPI, which is actually a weighted average of prices of tradable and nontradable goods. If these weights are known, it is easy to calculate the internal real exchange rate from the ratio of the CPI to the import price index (both expressed in terms of the domestic currency). Alternatively, it can be assumed that the weight of tradable goods in the CPI is equal to the average share of imports over total consumption—in line with the assumption that the import price is the price of tradable goods. The ratio of the CPI to the import price index can then be written

$$CPI/P_m = (P_m^y P_n^{1-y})/(P_m) = (P_n/P_m)^{1-y} = (RERN)^{1-y},$$

where $y$ is the weight of tradable goods in the CPI. Therefore,

$$RERN = (CPI/P_m)^{1/1-y}.$$

Figure 1 shows the GDP-weighted average external real exchange rate (ratio of domestic to foreign CPIs) for the WAEMU economies. The real exchange rate appreciated during most of the 1970s before depreciating between 1979 and 1984. It then appreciated between 1984 and 1986 without, however, reaching its 1979 level. It depreciated gradually during 1986–93 and sharply in 1994, but appreciated in the following years, partially offsetting the effect of the nominal exchange rate devaluation in 1994.

The internal real exchange rate in Figure 1 shows a substantial appreciation between 1985 and 1994, reversing the depreciation that occurred between 1980 and 1985. It reached its highest level in 1993, just before the devaluation. Finally, the devaluation of 1994 caused the internal real exchange rate to depreciate substantially in that year, although this effect was offset to some extent in the following years.

In addition to the effect of the devaluation of the CFA franc against the French franc in 1994, the real exchange rate of the WAEMU may also be influenced by the movement of the U.S. dollar against the French franc (Figure 2). The nominal exchange rate of the WAEMU in terms of the U.S. dollar (which reflects both factors) appreciated from 1985 to 1994. The two measures of the real exchange rate for the WAEMU show similar movements, although the internal real exchange rate exhibits fluctuations that are amplified by domestic price movements.

## Conclusions

This appendix constructed two measures of the real exchange rate in the WAEMU for the period 1970–97.

The external real exchange rate shows on average no appreciation of the real exchange rate before the devaluation of the nominal exchange rate in 1994, while the internal real exchange rate—which is thought to provide a better measure of competitiveness—shows a significant appreciation of the real exchange rate before 1994, as does the nominal exchange rate vis-à-vis the U.S. dollar. Both measures of the real exchange rate depreciated sharply in 1994 and appreciated somewhat thereafter, although the competitiveness gains achieved in 1994 have been largely preserved.

# Appendix III Determinants of Investment in the WAEMU

Capital investment, by increasing productive capacity and serving as a vehicle for new technologies, is an important engine of growth. It is thus encouraging that the share of investment in GDP has risen in every country of the WAEMU in recent years. However, the fact that the average investment ratio remains low in the WAEMU, compared not only with the developing countries of Asia, but also with the rest of sub-Saharan Africa, remains a source of concern (Table 3). Investment ratios vary widely within the WAEMU, from relatively high ratios in Burkina Faso and Mali to very low ones in Côte d'Ivoire, Togo, and, especially, Niger (Appendix IV, Table 10). The empirical tests presented in this appendix seek to explain these differences by using panel regressions to examine the determinants of annual investment (private plus public) in the period 1970–95 for the seven WAEMU countries for which data were available.

Several factors have been suggested as explaining investment behavior.[18] The traditional accelerator model suggests that changes in income should be positively associated with short-run fluctuations in investment. Other explanations of a more structural nature include demographic trends, the competitiveness and profitability of exports, and the attractiveness of the business environment. While difficult to measure, attractiveness of the business environment probably includes freedom from bureaucratic meddling and excessive regulation, as well as openness to the outside world through access to foreign goods and capital. Indeed, one of the advantages suggested for regional (and global) integration is that it may increase investment and hence growth. A related factor is the international competitiveness of domestic producers. The WAEMU countries experienced an appreciation of the real exchange rate in the late 1980s and early 1990s, which was associated with low investment, but investment rebounded after the devaluation of 1994. Finally, the price and profitability of the region's exports—which consist largely of primary commodities—could be expected to influence domestic investment. This relationship might be captured through the price ratio of primary commodities to manufactures.

The results of the panel regressions, using the average investment share of the WAEMU (*INV*) as the dependent variable during 1970–95, tend to confirm most of the hypotheses mentioned above. The growth variable (*GROW*) is not statistically significant (despite being biased upward, since positive investment probably also increases contemporaneous growth to some extent). However, the dependency ratio (*DEP*)—the ratio of the young and the elderly to those of working age; a measure of openness (*OPEN*)—exports plus imports divided by GDP; and two indices of "economic freedom" are significant. The economic freedom variables are subjective indicators[19] that measure the freedom of businesses to compete domestically (*COMPETE*) and the freedom of international capital transactions (*CAPITAL*). A simple average of the two variables for 1995 is reported in Table 3. In addition, the real effective exchange rate (*RER*), which is based on relative GDP deflators, has a significant negative effect on investment.[20] The regression did not include country dummies, and thus differences between countries that are not captured by the explanatory variables show up in the random error terms:

$$INV = \underset{(3.15)}{0.104}\ OPEN + \underset{(1.36)}{0.101}\ GROWTH$$

$$- \underset{(3.64)}{46.9}\ DEP + \underset{(3.31)}{5.49}\ COMPETE$$

$$+ \underset{(4.64)}{3.98}\ CAPITAL - \underset{(4.82)}{0.172}\ RER$$

Number of observations = 152
$R^2 = 0.37$
*t*-statistics are reported in parentheses below the coefficients.

---

[18]Some factors, like the cost of capital, could not be included in the analysis because no information is available for the WAEMU countries.

[19]Calculated by J. Gwartney, R. Lawson, and W. Block, *Economic Freedom of the World* (Vancouver, British Columbia, Canada: Fraser Institute, 1996).

[20]The price ratio of commodities to manufactures was not statistically significant, perhaps because it was correlated with other variables.

**Table 3. Investment Share, Trade Share, and Index of Economic Freedom in the WAEMU and Other Selected Countries, 1995**

(Percent)

| | Investment/ GDP | Imports + Exports/ GDP | Index of Economic Freedom[1] |
|---|---|---|---|
| WAEMU countries[2] | 15.8 | ... | ... |
| Benin | 19.3 | 64.0 | 2.5 |
| Burkina Faso | 24.0 | 44.7 | ... |
| Côte d'Ivoire | 12.8 | 75.9 | 2.0 |
| Mali | 26.0 | 38.2 | 3.5 |
| Niger | 7.2 | 30.1 | 2.5 |
| Senegal | 15.6 | 68.5 | 2.5 |
| Togo | 13.5 | 65.2 | 2.5 |
| Other African countries | 20.9 | ... | 2.5[3] |
| Selected other countries | | | |
| Brazil | 21.9 | 15.5 | 3.8 |
| France | 17.7 | 43.4 | 7.8 |
| India | 24.5 | 27.2 | 3.5 |
| Korea | 36.6 | 67.2 | 6.3 |
| United States | 16.5 | 24.4 | 10.0 |

Sources: IMF, World Economic Outlook database; World Bank, World Development Indicators database; and J. Gwartney, R. Lawson, and W. Block, *Economic Freedom of the World* (1996).

[1]Unweighted average of freedom of capital transactions and freedom of business to compete, for most recent year. A value of 0 is the least free, one of 10 is the most.

[2]Excluding Guinea-Bissau.

[3]Central African Republic, Chad, and Nigeria.

Additional explanatory variables were tried and some of those mentioned above were dropped, but generally the variables included remained statistically significant.[21] A Granger causality test was run, which confirmed that openness influenced investment rather than the reverse. The measure of openness is imperfect because larger countries tend to have lower ratios of trade to GDP than smaller ones for a given level of trade restrictiveness; inclusion of country size (as measured by GDP) in the regression still yielded a significant coefficient for the openness variable. Thus, there seems to be firm evidence that more freedom to compete and to access foreign goods and capital markets has favorable effects on the scale of investment in WAEMU countries, adding to evidence for other regions.[22]

[21]An exception was competitiveness, which, when measured by the relative *CPI* variable, changed the sign of the coefficient on the variable *COMPETE*.

[22]See for instance Ross Levine and David Renelt, "A Sensitivity Analysis of Cross-Country Growth Regressions," *American Economic Review*, Vol. 82 (September 1992), pp. 942–63; and Jeffrey Sachs and Andrew Warner, "Economic Reform and the Process of Global Integration," *Brookings Papers on Economic Activity:1,* Brookings Institution, 1995, pp. 1–118.

# Appendix IV    Background Tables

## Table 4.  WAEMU: Output Growth
*(Annual percentage changes)*

| | Average 1990–93 | 1994 | 1995 | 1996 | Prel. 1997 |
|---|---|---|---|---|---|
| | *(Real GDP)* | | | | |
| Benin | 2.8 | 4.4 | 4.6 | 5.6 | 5.3 |
| Burkina Faso | 2.6 | 1.2 | 3.8 | 6.2 | 5.5 |
| Côte d'Ivoire | −0.4 | 2.1 | 7.1 | 6.8 | 6.0 |
| Mali | 1.4 | 2.3 | 6.4 | 4.0 | 6.7 |
| Niger | −1.0 | 4.0 | 2.6 | 3.3 | 3.5 |
| Senegal | 0.9 | 2.9 | 4.8 | 5.7 | 5.2 |
| Togo | −5.9 | 16.8 | 6.8 | 8.2 | 4.8 |
| WAEMU[1] | 0.2 | 3.2 | 5.7 | 6.0 | 5.6 |
| | *(Per capita GDP)* | | | | |
| Benin | −0.3 | 1.5 | 2.9 | 1.5 | 2.1 |
| Burkina Faso | −0.3 | −1.6 | 0.9 | 3.4 | 2.5 |
| Côte d'Ivoire | −4.3 | −1.9 | 3.2 | 3.1 | 2.3 |
| Mali | −1.6 | −0.7 | 3.3 | 0.9 | 3.6 |
| Niger | −3.7 | 0.7 | −0.7 | 0.0 | 0.2 |
| Senegal | −1.9 | 0.1 | 2.1 | 3.0 | 2.5 |
| Togo | −8.4 | 13.2 | 3.5 | 5.0 | 1.7 |
| WAEMU[1] | −3.0 | −0.2 | 2.5 | 2.6 | 2.3 |

Sources: IMF staff estimates, and World Economic Outlook database, January 1998.

[1]Excluding Guinea-Bissau.

## Table 5.  WAEMU: Trade Volume Growth
*(Annual percentage changes)*

| | Average 1990–93 | 1994 | 1995 | 1996 | Prel. 1997 |
|---|---|---|---|---|---|
| | *(Export volume)* | | | | |
| Benin | 6.7 | 45.5 | 2.8 | 27.3 | 4.1 |
| Burkina Faso | 10.0 | 9.7 | 5.4 | 2.5 | 18.3 |
| Côte d'Ivoire | 4.4 | 4.9 | 6.0 | 21.7 | 3.9 |
| Mali | 8.7 | 1.4 | 19.6 | 2.6 | 31.7 |
| Niger | −2.9 | 2.0 | 6.8 | 11.9 | 18.3 |
| Senegal | 1.8 | 9.1 | 7.3 | 2.1 | 1.7 |
| Togo | −10.8 | 6.0 | 30.4 | 1.2 | 3.5 |
| WAEMU[1] | 3.6 | 8.8 | 8.6 | 13.0 | 8.8 |
| | *(Import volume)* | | | | |
| Benin | 1.7 | −32.3 | 39.0 | −0.9 | 3.0 |
| Burkina Faso | 7.1 | −29.9 | 24.4 | 12.8 | 5.8 |
| Côte d'Ivoire | −2.0 | −9.5 | 40.7 | 6.6 | 6.3 |
| Mali | 3.2 | −2.7 | 14.4 | 2.1 | 2.8 |
| Niger | −9.2 | −9.5 | 8.6 | −3.7 | 9.7 |
| Senegal | 0.2 | −4.4 | 5.0 | 4.2 | 2.9 |
| Togo | −13.7 | −16.1 | 56.6 | 8.0 | −2.1 |
| WAEMU[1] | −1.1 | −12.0 | 28.2 | 5.0 | 4.8 |

Sources: IMF staff estimates, and World Economic Outlook database, January 1998.

[1]Excluding Guinea-Bissau.

## Table 6. WAEMU: Real Effective Exchange Rates
*(Annual percentage changes)*

| | Average 1990–93 | 1994 | 1995 | 1996 | Prel. 1997 |
|---|---|---|---|---|---|
| Benin | 1.0 | −35.8 | 14.5 | 1.0 | 0.6 |
| Burkina Faso | −1.5 | −38.8 | 7.7 | 3.0 | −2.9 |
| Côte d'Ivoire | 0.2 | −34.5 | 8.3 | −1.0 | 2.2 |
| Mali | −2.4 | −38.1 | 12.6 | 3.6 | −6.9 |
| Niger | −4.9 | −33.5 | 10.9 | 3.3 | −3.0 |
| Senegal | −2.0 | −35.1 | 8.5 | −2.4 | −3.7 |
| Togo | −0.8 | −33.5 | 16.0 | 2.6 | 2.8 |
| WAEMU[1] | −1.1 | −35.4 | 9.8 | 0.3 | −0.8 |

Source: IMF staff estimates.
Note: In terms of relative consumer price indices.
[1]Excluding Guinea-Bissau.

## Table 7. WAEMU: Inflation
*(Annual percentage changes)*

| | Average 1990–93 | 1994 | 1995 | 1996 | Prel. 1997 |
|---|---|---|---|---|---|
| Benin | 2.4 | 38.6 | 14.9 | 4.7 | 3.8 |
| Burkina Faso | 0.2 | 24.7 | 7.8 | 6.1 | 2.3 |
| Côte d'Ivoire | 1.8 | 26.0 | 14.1 | 2.7 | 5.6 |
| Mali | −0.9 | 24.8 | 12.4 | 6.4 | — |
| Niger | −1.5 | 35.6 | 10.9 | 5.3 | 2.9 |
| Senegal | −0.6 | 32.1 | 8.5 | 2.8 | 1.8 |
| Togo | −0.1 | 35.3 | 15.9 | 4.6 | 8.2 |
| WAEMU[1] | 0.6 | 29.2 | 12.2 | 3.9 | 3.8 |

Sources: IMF staff estimates, and World Economic Outlook database, January 1998.
[1]Excluding Guinea-Bissau.

## Table 8. WAEMU: Fiscal Balances
*(Percent of GDP)*

| | Average 1990–93 | 1994 | 1995 | 1996 | Prel. 1997 |
|---|---|---|---|---|---|
| *(Primary balance)* | | | | | |
| Benin | −4.5 | −3.8 | −4.5 | −1.9 | −2.5 |
| Burkina Faso | −7.4 | −9.6 | −7.8 | −8.1 | −9.0 |
| Côte d'Ivoire | −2.6 | 1.4 | 3.2 | 3.8 | 3.0 |
| Mali | −8.4 | −11.4 | −9.1 | −6.9 | −7.8 |
| Niger | −7.8 | −10.2 | −5.5 | −3.7 | −5.3 |
| Senegal | −0.3 | −2.4 | 0.2 | 1.3 | 1.9 |
| Togo | −5.7 | −5.9 | −2.1 | −1.4 | 0.8 |
| WAEMU[1] | −3.9 | −3.4 | −1.2 | −0.2 | −0.7 |
| *(Overall balance, excluding grants)* | | | | | |
| Benin | −7.5 | −7.0 | −7.3 | −4.3 | −4.2 |
| Burkina Faso | −8.8 | −11.0 | −9.2 | −9.0 | −9.8 |
| Côte d'Ivoire | −12.5 | −7.2 | −4.4 | −2.8 | −2.7 |
| Mali | −10.3 | −13.7 | −10.5 | −7.9 | −8.8 |
| Niger | −9.7 | −12.5 | −7.8 | −5.4 | −6.8 |
| Senegal | −2.6 | −6.1 | −3.5 | −2.2 | −1.5 |
| Togo | −9.1 | −13.1 | −7.8 | −6.3 | −3.6 |
| WAEMU[1] | −9.1 | −8.7 | −6.0 | −4.3 | −4.3 |

Sources: IMF staff estimates, and World Economic Outlook database, January 1998.
[1]Excluding Guinea-Bissau.

## Table 9. WAEMU: Government Revenue, Excluding Grants
*(Percent of GDP)*

| | Average 1990–93 | 1994 | 1995 | 1996 | Prel. 1997 |
|---|---|---|---|---|---|
| Benin | 11.7 | 12.8 | 14.9 | 15.2 | 14.6 |
| Burkina Faso | 12.5 | 11.0 | 11.8 | 12.3 | 13.0 |
| Côte d'Ivoire | 19.6 | 19.9 | 22.1 | 22.5 | 22.2 |
| Mali | 15.2 | 12.2 | 13.1 | 14.4 | 14.4 |
| Niger | 8.6 | 6.1 | 7.2 | 7.8 | 8.4 |
| Senegal | 18.0 | 14.9 | 16.3 | 16.0 | 16.3 |
| Togo | 16.8 | 12.1 | 14.7 | 14.8 | 15.2 |
| WAEMU[1] | 16.4 | 15.2 | 17.0 | 17.4 | 17.4 |

Sources: IMF staff estimates, and World Economic Outlook database, January 1998.
[1]Excluding Guinea-Bissau.

## Table 10. WAEMU: Gross Domestic Investment
*(Percent of GDP)*

|  | Average 1990–93 | 1994 | 1995 | 1996 | Prel. 1997 |
|---|---|---|---|---|---|
| Benin | 14.5 | 15.8 | 19.6 | 17.1 | 17.8 |
| Burkina Faso | 20.6 | 19.3 | 22.5 | 24.8 | 26.2 |
| Côte d'Ivoire | 6.9 | 11.1 | 12.9 | 13.9 | 16.0 |
| Mali | 22.3 | 26.0 | 26.0 | 26.5 | 25.8 |
| Niger | 7.1 | 10.4 | 7.5 | 9.7 | 9.7 |
| Senegal | 13.3 | 16.2 | 16.9 | 17.4 | 18.7 |
| Togo | 15.9 | 15.1 | 16.1 | 16.3 | 15.2 |
| WAEMU[1] | 12.1 | 14.8 | 16.2 | 16.9 | 18.1 |

Sources: IMF staff estimates, and World Economic Outlook database, January 1998.
[1] Excluding Guinea-Bissau.

## Table 11. WAEMU: Gross Domestic Saving
*(Percent of GDP)*

|  | Average 1990–93 | 1994 | 1995 | 1996 | Prel. 1997 |
|---|---|---|---|---|---|
| Benin | 5.2 | 9.5 | 10.2 | 8.7 | 9.9 |
| Burkina Faso | 6.5 | 6.1 | 7.1 | 7.5 | 9.2 |
| Côte d'Ivoire | 10.1 | 22.4 | 20.3 | 22.3 | 23.1 |
| Mali | 5.9 | 7.1 | 9.5 | 10.8 | 14.2 |
| Niger | 2.2 | 1.7 | 0.4 | 3.1 | 2.1 |
| Senegal | 6.1 | 9.6 | 11.3 | 11.9 | 13.2 |
| Togo | 6.6 | 11.4 | 11.9 | 11.4 | 11.2 |
| WAEMU[1] | 7.3 | 13.6 | 13.5 | 14.6 | 15.7 |

Sources: IMF staff estimates, and World Economic Outlook database, January 1998.
[1] Excluding Guinea-Bissau.

## Table 12. WAEMU: External Current Account Balance, Excluding Grants
*(Percent of GDP)*

|  | Average 1990–93 | 1994 | 1995 | 1996 | Prel. 1997 |
|---|---|---|---|---|---|
| Benin | −6.9 | −5.2 | −8.2 | −6.8 | −6.5 |
| Burkina Faso | −10.3 | −8.7 | −11.3 | −13.4 | −13.3 |
| Côte d'Ivoire | −12.8 | −2.2 | −7.2 | −6.0 | −5.6 |
| Mali | −14.5 | −16.9 | −15.3 | −14.7 | −10.8 |
| Niger | −8.7 | −13.6 | −11.1 | −9.2 | −10.0 |
| Senegal | −9.9 | −9.9 | −9.2 | −7.7 | −7.5 |
| Togo | −10.5 | −8.1 | −6.7 | −6.2 | −5.3 |
| WAEMU[1] | −11.2 | −7.2 | −9.1 | −8.2 | −7.6 |

Sources: IMF staff estimates, and World Economic Outlook database, January 1998.
[1] Excluding Guinea-Bissau.

## Table 13. WAEMU: Public External Debt
*(Percent of GDP)*

|  | Average 1990–93 | 1994 | 1995 | 1996 | Prel. 1997 |
|---|---|---|---|---|---|
| Benin | 65.5 | 102.3 | 78.5 | 70.2 | 63.1 |
| Burkina Faso | 18.4 | 74.3 | 52.3 | 50.7 | 56.4 |
| Côte d'Ivoire | 124.9 | 183.9 | 157.9 | 154.7 | 140.3 |
| Mali | 100.5 | 141.0 | 115.4 | 108.4 | 113.9 |
| Niger | 55.0 | 84.8 | 74.5 | 68.5 | 73.7 |
| Senegal | 56.1 | 80.9 | 76.6 | 77.3 | 73.0 |
| Togo | 81.1 | 131.7 | 108.3 | 99.4 | 93.8 |
| WAEMU[1] | 85.0 | 132.2 | 113.1 | 109.3 | 103.3 |

Sources: IMF staff estimates, and World Economic Outlook database, January 1998.
[1] Excluding Guinea-Bissau.

## Table 14. WAEMU: Balance of Payments
*(Billions of CFA francs)*

|  | 1994 | 1995 | 1996 | Prel. 1997 |
|---|---|---|---|---|
| Exports (f.o.b.) | 2,878.7 | 3,298.4 | 3,654.1 | 3,960.1 |
| Imports (f.o.b.) | −2,485.8 | −3,118.2 | −3,166.2 | −3,473.1 |
| Trade balance | 392.9 | 180.2 | 487.9 | 487.0 |
| Services | −1,108.7 | −1,296.5 | −1,258.6 | −1,317.7 |
| Transfers | 1,017.6 | 810.9 | 572.1 | 535.4 |
| Private | −56.4 | −71.4 | −87.2 | −111.0 |
| Official | 1,074.0 | 882.3 | 659.3 | 646.4 |
| Current balance[1] | −772.2 | −1,187.7 | −857.9 | −941.7 |
| Capital account | 435.8 | 183.9 | 19.1 | 497.3 |
| Private | 179.5 | 108.7 | −93.5 | 167.3 |
| Public | 256.3 | 75.2 | 112.6 | 330.0 |
| Errors and omissions | −31.6 | −26.3 | −22.0 | — |
| Overall balance | 706.0 | −147.8 | −201.5 | 202.0 |
| Financing | −706.0 | 147.8 | 201.5 | −202.0 |
| Change in arrears | −666.6 | −155.7 | −29.0 | −207.0 |
| Debt relief | 843.6 | 313.6 | 355.6 | 101.2 |
| Other (including change in foreign assets) | −883.0 | −10.1 | −125.1 | −96.2 |
| Exports + imports/GDP | 51.14064 | 52.80631 | 50.68368 | 50.44656 |
| Trade balance/GDP | 3.745579 | 1.482981 | 3.62573 | 3.305101 |
| Current account balance/GDP | −7.36151 | −9.77434 | −6.37531 | −6.39099 |
| GDP | 10,489.7 | 12,151.2 | 13,456.6 | 14,734.8 |

Source: BCEAO.

Note: Data are provided by the BCEAO and may show differences with data from the World Economic Outlook database.

[1]Excluding official transfers.

## Table 15. WAEMU Governments' Financial Operations
*(Billions of CFA francs)*

| | 1994 | 1995 | 1996 | Prel. 1997 |
|---|---|---|---|---|
| Total revenue and grants | 2,025.6 | 2,491.9 | 2,805.1 | 3,058.1 |
| Total revenue | 1,625.9 | 2,093.8 | 2,378.0 | 2,648.3 |
| Tax revenue | 1,352.3 | 1,756.1 | 2,048.0 | 2,254.9 |
| Direct taxes | 304.3 | 441.7 | 524.8 | 603.8 |
| Indirect taxes | 1,019.8 | 1,290.6 | 1,495.2 | 1,615.3 |
| Taxes on goods and services | 266.5 | 335.7 | 405.3 | 446.1 |
| Taxes on foreign trade | 753.3 | 954.9 | 1,089.9 | 1,169.2 |
| Other taxes | 28.2 | 23.8 | 28.0 | 35.8 |
| Nontax revenue | 273.6 | 337.7 | 330.0 | 393.4 |
| Grants | 399.7 | 398.1 | 427.1 | 409.8 |
| Total expenditure | 2,559.3 | 2,833.5 | 2,972.3 | 3,245.1 |
| Current expenditure | 1,926.8 | 2,026.6 | 2,091.7 | 2,189.7 |
| Wages and salaries | 721.6 | 769.3 | 818.2 | 854.1 |
| Interest due | 534.7 | 514.3 | 476.0 | 471.9 |
| Domestic interest | 70.5 | 64.2 | 56.4 | 69.4 |
| Foreign interest | 464.2 | 450.1 | 419.6 | 402.5 |
| Other current expenditure | 670.5 | 743.0 | 797.5 | 863.7 |
| Capital expenditure | 639.6 | 812.5 | 881.4 | 1,044.0 |
| Domestically financed | 153.5 | 254.4 | 265.1 | 355.0 |
| Externally financed | 486.1 | 558.1 | 616.3 | 689.0 |
| Net lending | −7.1 | −5.6 | −0.8 | 11.4 |
| Primary balance[1] | 80.3 | 327.1 | 497.2 | 575.5 |
| Overall balance, excluding grants | −933.4 | −739.7 | −594.3 | −596.8 |
| Overall balance | −533.7 | −341.6 | −167.2 | −187.0 |
| Financing | 533.7 | 341.6 | 167.2 | 187.0 |
| Domestic financing | −155.8 | −119.7 | −237.3 | −215.5 |
| Arrears | −67.2 | −106.9 | −188.8 | −112.7 |
| Banking system | −15.8 | 21.4 | −100.3 | −50.5 |
| Nonbank borrowing | −72.8 | −34.2 | 51.8 | −52.3 |
| External financing | 689.5 | 461.3 | 404.5 | 272.3 |
| Drawings | 866.7 | 692.9 | 600.7 | 591.3 |
| Amortization due | −615.9 | −610.0 | −530.9 | −451.5 |
| Debt relief | 973.9 | 457.1 | 349.7 | 226.8 |
| Arrears | −535.2 | −78.7 | −15.0 | −94.3 |
| | *(Percent of GDP)* | | | |
| Budgetary revenue | 15.5 | 17.2 | 17.7 | 18.0 |
| Total expenditure | 24.4 | 23.3 | 22.1 | 22.0 |
| Current expenditure | 18.4 | 16.7 | 15.6 | 14.9 |
| Capital expenditure | 6.1 | 6.7 | 6.5 | 7.1 |
| Primary balance | 0.8 | 2.7 | 3.7 | 3.9 |
| Overall balance excluding grants | −8.9 | −6.1 | −4.4 | −4.1 |
| *Memorandum items* | *(Percent of tax revenue)* | | | |
| Wages/tax revenue | 53.4 | 43.8 | 40.0 | 37.9 |
| Domestically financed investment/tax revenue | 11.4 | 14.5 | 12.9 | 15.7 |
| Primary balance/tax revenue | 5.9 | 18.6 | 24.3 | 25.5 |

Source: BCEAO.

Note: Data are provided by the BCEAO and may show differences with data from the World Economic Outlook database.

[1] Total revenue less total expenditure excluding interest due, externally financed investment, and net lending.

## Table 16. WAEMU: Monetary Survey
*(Billions of CFA francs)*

| | 1993 Dec.[1] | 1994 Dec.[1] | 1995 Dec.[1] | 1995 Dec. | 1996 Sept. | 1996 Dec. | 1997 Mar. | 1997 Jun. | 1997 Sept. | Prel. 1997 Dec. |
|---|---|---|---|---|---|---|---|---|---|---|
| Net foreign assets | −225 | 430 | 693 | 733 | 711 | 870 | 1,248 | 1,133 | 1,071 | 1,088 |
| Gross foreign assets | 306 | 1,444 | 1,816 | 1,813 | 1,828 | 2,003 | 2,376 | 2,302 | 2,353 | 2,278 |
| Liabilities | 531 | 1,013 | 1,123 | 1,080 | 1,117 | 1,133 | 1,128 | 1,168 | 1,282 | 1,190 |
| Net domestic assets | 2,217 | 2,345 | 2,473 | 2,322 | 2,426 | 2,532 | 2,401 | 2,363 | 2,392 | 2,566 |
| Net credit to government | 430 | 897 | 986 | 1,053 | 1,008 | 946 | 1,016 | 1,134 | 1,117 | 1,011 |
| Credit to economy | 1,764 | 1,607 | 1,861 | 1,746 | 1,844 | 2,044 | 2,087 | 2,012 | 2,007 | 2,251 |
| Crop credits | 97 | 190 | 248 | 248 | 124 | 196 | 295 | 222 | 161 | 287 |
| Other credits | 1,667 | 1,416 | 1,613 | 1,498 | 1,720 | 1,847 | 1,791 | 1,790 | 1,847 | 1,964 |
| Other items (net) | 23 | −159 | −373 | −477 | −427 | −458 | −702 | −783 | −732 | −696 |
| Money supply | 1,992 | 2,776 | 3,166 | 3,055 | 3,137 | 3,401 | 3,649 | 3,496 | 3,464 | 3,654 |
| Currency in circulation | 593 | 894 | 1,018 | 1,018 | 908 | 1,060 | 1,163 | 1,072 | 1,007 | 1,217 |
| Postal deposits | 10 | 14 | 14 | 14 | 19 | 17 | 18 | 16 | 16 | 18 |
| Savings banks | 11 | 13 | 15 | 15 | 17 | 18 | 18 | 19 | 19 | 19 |
| Bank deposits | 1,378 | 1,855 | 2,118 | 2,008 | 2,192 | 2,307 | 2,450 | 2,389 | 2,422 | 2,400 |
| Public enterprises | 188 | 254 | 331 | 309 | 313 | 343 | 381 | 359 | 382 | 368 |
| Sight deposits | 119 | 174 | 215 | 198 | 209 | 226 | 252 | 248 | 231 | 221 |
| Term deposits | 69 | 80 | 117 | 111 | 104 | 117 | 129 | 111 | 150 | 147 |
| Private sector | 1,191 | 1,601 | 1,787 | 1,699 | 1,880 | 1,963 | 2,069 | 2,030 | 2,040 | 2,032 |
| Sight deposits | 512 | 816 | 908 | 864 | 881 | 977 | 1,040 | 985 | 982 | 1,020 |
| Term deposits | 678 | 784 | 879 | 835 | 999 | 986 | 1,029 | 1,044 | 1,058 | 1,011 |
| | | | | *(Twelve-month rate of increase; percent)* | | | | | | |
| *Memorandum items* | | | | | | | | | | |
| Net foreign assets | ... | 291 | 61 | ... | ... | 19 | ... | ... | 51 | 25 |
| Net domestic assets | ... | 6 | 5 | ... | ... | 9 | ... | ... | −1 | 1 |
| Net credit to government | ... | 109 | 10 | ... | ... | −10 | ... | ... | 11 | 7 |
| Credit to economy | ... | −9 | 16 | ... | ... | 17 | ... | ... | 9 | 10 |
| Money supply | ... | 39 | 14 | ... | ... | 11 | ... | ... | 10 | 7 |
| Currency in circulation | ... | 51 | 14 | ... | ... | 4 | ... | ... | 11 | 15 |
| Bank deposits | ... | 35 | 14 | ... | ... | 15 | ... | ... | 10 | 4 |

Source: BCEAO.

[1]Includes data for liquidated banks.

## Table 17. WAEMU: Summary Accounts of the Central Bank
*(Billions of CFA francs)*

| | 1993 Dec.[1] | 1994 Dec.[1] | 1995 Dec.[1] | 1995 Dec. | 1996 Sept. | 1996 Dec. | 1997 Mar. | 1997 Jun. | 1997 Sept. | Prel. Dec. 1997 |
|---|---|---|---|---|---|---|---|---|---|---|
| **Assets** | | | | | | | | | | |
| Net foreign assets | −134 | 372 | 609 | 609 | 617 | 755 | 1,061 | 970 | 941 | 962 |
| Gross foreign assets | 190 | 1,138 | 1,417 | 1,417 | 1,455 | 1,612 | 1,938 | 1,894 | 1,965 | 1,889 |
| Liabilities[2] | 325 | 767 | 809 | 809 | 837 | 857 | 877 | 925 | 1,024 | 927 |
| Net domestic assets | 1,135 | 826 | 698 | 697 | 551 | 580 | 351 | 452 | 420 | 525 |
| Net credit to government | 535 | 792 | 782 | 782 | 756 | 745 | 769 | 855 | 831 | 797 |
| Guaranteed bonds | 360 | 317 | 270 | 272 | 328 | 296 | 299 | 334 | 312 | 326 |
| Securitized debt | — | 209 | 117 | 117 | 1 | 38 | 7 | 7 | 7 | 19 |
| Other (including IMF) | 233 | 399 | 550 | 517 | 608 | 642 | 776 | 764 | 791 | 777 |
| Government deposits | 60 | 136 | 158 | 158 | 180 | 231 | 314 | 249 | 279 | 325 |
| Net claims on banks and financial institutions | 809 | 157 | 164 | 164 | 76 | 162 | 80 | 83 | 54 | 174 |
| Money market paper | 192 | 29 | 53 | — | — | — | — | — | — | — |
| Repurchase agreements (pensions) | 19 | — | 10 | — | — | — | — | — | — | — |
| Collateralized loans | 148 | 121 | 100 | — | — | — | — | — | — | — |
| Other | 450 | 7 | — | — | — | — | — | — | — | — |
| Other items (net) | −209 | −123 | −248 | −249 | −281 | −327 | −498 | −485 | −465 | −446 |
| **Liabilities** | | | | | | | | | | |
| Base money | 1,001 | 1,197 | 1,306 | 1,306 | 1,169 | 1,335 | 1,412 | 1,422 | 1,361 | 1,487 |
| Currency in circulation | 593 | 894 | 1,018 | 1,018 | 908 | 1,060 | 1,163 | 1,072 | 1,007 | 1,217 |
| Bank deposits | 340 | 220 | 193 | 193 | 168 | 180 | 148 | 253 | 250 | 168 |
| Other deposits | 67 | 84 | 95 | 95 | 93 | 96 | 101 | 97 | 104 | 102 |
| *Memorandum item* Gross foreign assets/base money (in percent) | 19 | 95 | 108 | 109 | 124 | 121 | 137 | 133 | 144 | 127 |

Source: BCEAO.
[1]Includes data for liquidated banks.
[2]Includes liabilities to IMF.

## Table 18. WAEMU: Summary Accounts of the Commercial Banks
*(Billions of CFA francs)*

| | 1993 Dec.[1] | 1994 Dec.[1] | 1995 Dec.[1] | 1995 Dec. | 1996 Sept. | 1996 Dec. | 1997 Mar. | 1997 Jun. | 1997 Sept. | Prel. 1997 Dec. |
|---|---|---|---|---|---|---|---|---|---|---|
| **Assets** | | | | | | | | | | |
| Net foreign assets[2] | −91 | 59 | 85 | 124 | 94 | 115 | 187 | 164 | 130 | 126 |
| Gross foreign assets | 115 | 305 | 399 | 396 | 373 | 391 | 438 | 407 | 388 | 389 |
| Liabilities | 206 | 247 | 314 | 272 | 279 | 276 | 251 | 244 | 257 | 263 |
| Net domestic assets | 1,849 | 1,662 | 1,923 | 1,773 | 1,910 | 2,066 | 2,087 | 2,021 | 2,012 | 2,142 |
| Net credit to government | −102 | 112 | 200 | 267 | 240 | 196 | 234 | 264 | 273 | 208 |
| Claims | 283 | 623 | 724 | 701 | 847 | 827 | 800 | 824 | 848 | 807 |
| Of which, securitized debt | — | 201 | 289 | 289 | 367 | 331 | 341 | 341 | 320 | 320 |
| Deposits | 385 | 511 | 524 | 434 | 607 | 631 | 566 | 559 | 575 | 599 |
| Credit to economy | 1,726 | 1,566 | 1,821 | 1,707 | 1,805 | 1,998 | 2,048 | 1,977 | 1,971 | 2,204 |
| Short-term credits | 868 | 944 | 1,118 | 1,048 | 1,077 | 1,247 | 1,320 | 1,224 | 1,222 | 1,426 |
| Crop credits | 97 | 190 | 248 | 248 | 124 | 197 | 295 | 222 | 161 | 287 |
| Ordinary credits | 771 | 754 | 870 | 801 | 953 | 1,051 | 1,024 | 1,002 | 1,062 | 1,139 |
| Medium-term credits | 568 | 459 | 549 | 516 | 580 | 605 | 589 | 614 | 612 | 641 |
| Long-term credits | 290 | 163 | 154 | 142 | 148 | 146 | 139 | 139 | 137 | 137 |
| Other items net | 225 | −16 | −98 | −201 | −135 | −128 | −195 | −220 | −232 | −270 |
| Reserves[3] | 344 | 200 | 177 | 177 | 157 | 178 | 146 | 192 | 211 | 188 |
| **Liabilities** | | | | | | | | | | |
| Private sector and public enterprise deposits | 1,311 | 1,771 | 2,023 | 1,913 | 2,099 | 2,211 | 2,349 | 2,314 | 2,318 | 2,297 |
| Public enterprises | 139 | 193 | 263 | 240 | 249 | 278 | 310 | 293 | 310 | 295 |
| Private sector | 1,172 | 1,578 | 1,761 | 1,673 | 1,850 | 1,933 | 2,039 | 2,021 | 2,007 | 2,003 |
| Central bank loans | 791 | 150 | 162 | 162 | 62 | 148 | 70 | 63 | 36 | 159 |
| *Memorandum items* | | | | | *(Percent of deposits)* | | | | | |
| Bank reserves | 20 | 9 | 7 | 8 | 6 | 6 | 5 | 7 | 7 | 6 |
| Securitized debt | — | 9 | 11 | 12 | 14 | 12 | 12 | 12 | 11 | 11 |
| Liquid assets | 20 | 18 | 18 | 20 | 19 | 18 | 17 | 19 | 18 | 18 |
| Loans/deposits | 96 | 65 | 68 | 72 | 62 | 66 | 67 | 66 | 66 | 72 |
| Reserves + securitized debt/deposits | 20 | 18 | 18 | 20 | 19 | 18 | 17 | 19 | 18 | 18 |

Source: BCEAO.
[1]Includes data for liquidated banks.
[2]Excluding all intra-WAEMU claims and liabilities, including securitized debt of governments.
[3]Including deposits with central bank, currency in vaults, and BCEAO short-term bonds.

# Table 19. WAEMU: Indicators of Banking Sector Soundness

| | Number of Active Banks | | | | Number of Banks Not Meeting Prudential Ratios | | | | | | | | Share of Non-performing Assets[1] | | | | Number of Banks with Government Share Exceeding 20 Percent | |
| | | | | | Solvency | | | | Liquidity | | | | | | | | | |
| | 1993 | 1994 | 1995 | 1996 | 1993 | 1994 | 1995 | 1996 | 1993 | 1994 | 1995 | 1996 | 1993 | 1994 | 1995 | 1996 | Dec. 1995 | Dec. 1996 |
|---|---|---|---|---|---|---|---|---|---|---|---|---|---|---|---|---|---|---|
| Benin | 5 | 5 | 5 | 5 | 0 | 1 | 2 | 1 | 0 | 0 | 0 | 2 | 9.3 | 7.4 | 6.9 | 3.6 | 0 | 0 |
| Including provisions[2] | | | | | | | | | | | | | 16.0 | 16.4 | 15.4 | 10.0 | | |
| Burkina Faso | 8 | 8 | 5 | 5 | 5 | 4 | 0 | 2 | 1 | 1 | 0 | 1 | 15.2 | 8.4 | 5.6 | 2.9 | 4 | 5 |
| Including provisions[2] | | | | | | | | | | | | | 34.3 | 29.9 | 19.8 | 11.0 | | |
| Côte d'Ivoire | 14 | 14 | 15 | 15 | 3 | 6 | 3 | 0 | 3 | 4 | 1 | 5 | 16.2 | 9.9 | 4.6 | 5.8 | 4 | 3 |
| Including provisions[2] | | | | | | | | | | | | | 32.8 | 31.2 | 21.2 | 19.7 | | |
| Mali | 7 | 7 | 7 | 7 | 3 | 3 | 3 | 4 | 1 | 0 | 0 | 1 | 28.1 | 32.0 | 18.3 | 10.7 | 4 | 4 |
| Including provisions[2] | | | | | | | | | | | | | 45.9 | 52.5 | 34.7 | 24.8 | | |
| Niger | 6 | 6 | 5 | 5 | 2 | 1 | 2 | 1 | 1 | 1 | 2 | 2 | 28.6 | 7.5 | 4.0 | 5.0 | 2 | 2 |
| Including provisions[2] | | | | | | | | | | | | | 55.0 | 43.0 | 39.5 | 29.8 | | |
| Senegal | 9 | 9 | 8 | 9 | 5 | 3 | 3 | 2 | 6 | 2 | 3 | 4 | 9.9 | 11.1 | 11.8 | 7.5 | 4 | 4 |
| Including provisions[2] | | | | | | | | | | | | | 22.5 | 24.8 | 24.2 | 19.6 | | |
| Togo | 7 | 7 | 7 | 7 | 0 | 4 | 4 | 3 | 0 | 4 | 3 | 3 | 17.2 | 18.1 | 15.8 | 5.3 | 4 | 6 |
| Including provisions[2] | | | | | | | | | | | | | 33.4 | 35.4 | 29.1 | 19.4 | | |
| **Total** | 56 | 56 | 52 | 53 | 18 | 22 | 17 | 13 | 12 | 12 | 9 | 18 | 15.8 | 12.0 | 7.9 | 6.2 | 22 | 24 |
| Including provisions[2] | | | | | | | | | | | | | 32.2 | 31.6 | 23.7 | 19.6 | | |

Source: WAEMU, Annual Report of the Banking Commission (1996).
[1] In percent of credit to the economy, unless otherwise indicated.
[2] Total amount of bad loans (that is, including provisions) over total credit.

## Table 20. WAEMU: Convergence Criteria

| | 1993 | 1994 | 1995 | 1996 | 1997 | Prel. 1997 |
|---|---|---|---|---|---|---|
| | | | (Percentage of tax revenue) | | | |
| **Wage bill/tax revenue (<50 percent )** | | | | | | |
| Benin | 57 | 50 | 44 | 41 | 43 | 43 |
| Burkina Faso | 72 | 56 | 48 | 43 | 39 | 39 |
| Côte d'Ivoire | 72 | 48 | 39 | 37 | 37 | 37 |
| Mali | 49 | 43 | 37 | 29 | 31 | 30 |
| Niger | 97 | 102 | 80 | 50 | 57 | ... |
| Senegal | 60 | 56 | 48 | 44 | 41 | 41 |
| Togo | 125 | 95 | 64 | 57 | 51 | 51 |
| WAEMU | 69 | 54 | 44 | 40 | ... | ... |
| **Public investment paid from domestic revenue/tax revenue (>20 percent)** | | | | | | |
| Benin | 5 | 5 | 11 | 6 | 11 | 11 |
| Burkina Faso | 12 | 9 | 8 | 10 | 17 | 17 |
| Côte d'Ivoire | 10 | 14 | 18 | 16 | 19 | 19 |
| Mali | 11 | 13 | 14 | 14 | 14 | 14 |
| Niger | 3 | 6 | 4 | 4 | 7 | ... |
| Senegal | 13 | 10 | 11 | 11 | 12 | 12 |
| Togo | 19 | 5 | 8 | 5 | 4 | 4 |
| WAEMU | 11 | 11 | 14 | 13 | ... | ... |
| **Primary fiscal balance/tax revenue (>15 percent )** | | | | | | |
| Benin | 20 | 19 | 19 | 27 | 20 | 20 |
| Burkina Faso | −34 | — | 9 | 14 | 17 | 17 |
| Côte d'Ivoire | −22 | 19 | 27 | 30 | 27 | 27 |
| Mali | −72 | 17 | 32 | 40 | 33 | 33 |
| Niger | −118 | −98 | −29 | 5 | −4 | ... |
| Senegal | −13 | 11 | 24 | 26 | 31 | 31 |
| Togo | −123 | −53 | −13 | −11 | 6 | 6 |
| WAEMU | −30 | 8 | 21 | 26 | ... | ... |
| | | | (Billions of CFA francs) | | | |
| **Change in external arrears (≤0)** | | | | | | |
| Benin | 2 | −3 | — | — | — | — |
| Burkina Faso | 3 | −15 | −4 | — | ... | — |
| Côte d'Ivoire | 269 | −353 | 7 | 2 | — | — |
| Mali | 5 | −20 | — | — | — | — |
| Niger | 19 | −67 | 34 | −26 | 2 | ... |
| Senegal | 37 | −129 | −46 | — | −9 | −9 |
| Togo | 20 | 16 | 1 | −3 | −47 | −47 |
| WAEMU | 355 | −570 | −7 | −27 | −53 | −55 |
| **Change in domestic arrears (≤0)** | | | | | | |
| Benin | −10 | −11 | −17 | −26 | −13 | −13 |
| Burkina Faso | — | −7 | −16 | −19 | — | — |
| Côte d'Ivoire | −27 | −98 | −79 | −84 | −78 | −78 |
| Mali | 4 | −10 | −14 | −19 | −4 | −4 |
| Niger | 6 | 6 | −12 | −20 | −21 | ... |
| Senegal | 12 | −32 | −15 | — | −9 | — |
| Togo | 29 | −6 | −6 | 2 | −25 | −24 |
| WAEMU | 14 | −157 | −159 | −165 | −150 | −119 |

Sources: IMF staff estimates; and WAEMU regional Banking Commission.

## Recent Occasional Papers of the International Monetary Fund

170. The West African Economic and Monetary Union: Recent Developments and Policy Issues, by a Staff Team led by Ernesto Hernández-Catá and comprising Christian A. François, Paul Masson, Pascal Bouvier, Patrick Peroz, Dominique Desruelle, and Athanasios Vamvakidis. 1998.

169. Financial Sector Development in Sub-Saharan African Countries, by Hassanali Mehran, Piero Ugolini, Jean Phillipe Briffaux, George Iden, Tonny Lybek, Stephen Swaray, and Peter Hayward. 1998.

168. Exit Strategies: Policy Options for Countries Seeking Greater Exchange Rate Flexibility, by a staff team led by Barry Eichengreen and Paul Masson with Hugh Bredenkamp, Barry Johnston, Javier Hamann, Esteban Jadresic, and Inci Ötker. 1998.

167. Exchange Rate Assessment: Extensions of the Macroeconomic Balance Approach, edited by Peter Isard and Hamid Faruqee. 1998

166. Hedge Funds and Financial Market Dynamics, by a staff team led by Barry Eichengreen and Donald Mathieson with Bankim Chadha, Anne Jansen, Laura Kodres, and Sunil Sharma. 1998.

165. Algeria: Stabilization and Transition to the Market, by Karim Nashashibi, Patricia Alonso-Gamo, Stefania Bazzoni, Alain Féler, Nicole Laframboise, and Sebastian Paris Horvitz. 1998.

164. MULTIMOD Mark III: The Core Dynamic and Steady-State Model, by Douglas Laxton, Peter Isard, Hamid Faruqee, Eswar Prasad, and Bart Turtelboom. 1998.

163. Egypt: Beyond Stabilization, Toward a Dynamic Market Economy, by a staff team led by Howard Handy. 1998.

162. Fiscal Policy Rules, by George Kopits and Steven Symansky. 1998.

161. The Nordic Banking Crises: Pitfalls in Financial Liberalization? by Burkhard Dress and Ceyla Pazarbaşıoğlu. 1998.

160. Fiscal Reform in Low-Income Countries: Experience Under IMF-Supported Programs, by a staff team led by George T. Abed and comprising Liam Ebrill, Sanjeev Gupta, Benedict Clements, Ronald McMorran, Anthony Pellechio, Jerald Schiff, and Marijn Verhoeven. 1998.

159. Hungary: Economic Policies for Sustainable Growth, Carlo Cottarelli, Thomas Krueger, Reza Moghadam, Perry Perone, Edgardo Ruggiero, and Rachel van Elkan. 1998.

158. Transparency in Government Operations, by George Kopits and Jon Craig. 1998.

157. Central Bank Reforms in the Baltics, Russia, and the Other Countries of the Former Soviet Union, by a staff team led by Malcolm Knight and comprising Susana Almuiña, John Dalton, Inci Otker, Ceyla Pazarbaşıoğlu, Arne B. Petersen, Peter Quirk, Nicholas M. Roberts, Gabriel Sensenbrenner, and Jan Willem van der Vossen. 1997.

156. The ESAF at Ten Years: Economic Adjustment and Reform in Low-Income Countries, by the staff of the International Monetary Fund. 1997.

155. Fiscal Policy Issues During the Transition in Russia, by Augusto Lopez-Claros and Sergei V. Alexashenko. 1998.

154. Credibility Without Rules? Monetary Frameworks in the Post–Bretton Woods Era, by Carlo Cottarelli and Curzio Giannini. 1997.

153. Pension Regimes and Saving, by G.A. Mackenzie, Philip Gerson, and Alfredo Cuevas. 1997.

152. Hong Kong, China: Growth, Structural Change, and Economic Stability During the Transition, by John Dodsworth and Dubravko Mihaljek. 1997.

151. Currency Board Arrangements: Issues and Experiences, by a staff team led by Tomás J.T. Baliño and Charles Enoch. 1997.

150. Kuwait: From Reconstruction to Accumulation for Future Generations, by Nigel Andrew Chalk, Mohamed A. El-Erian, Susan J. Fennell, Alexei P. Kireyev, and John F. Wilson. 1997.

149. The Composition of Fiscal Adjustment and Growth: Lessons from Fiscal Reforms in Eight Economies, by G.A. Mackenzie, David W.H. Orsmond, and Philip R. Gerson. 1997.

148. Nigeria: Experience with Structural Adjustment, by Gary Moser, Scott Rogers, and Reinold van Til, with Robin Kibuka and Inutu Lukonga. 1997.

147. Aging Populations and Public Pension Schemes, by Sheetal K. Chand and Albert Jaeger. 1996.

146. Thailand: The Road to Sustained Growth, by Kalpana Kochhar, Louis Dicks-Mireaux, Balazs Horvath, Mauro Mecagni, Erik Offerdal, and Jianping Zhou. 1996.

145. Exchange Rate Movements and Their Impact on Trade and Investment in the APEC Region, by Takatoshi Ito, Peter Isard, Steven Symansky, and Tamim Bayoumi. 1996.

144. National Bank of Poland: The Road to Indirect Instruments, by Piero Ugolini. 1996.

143. Adjustment for Growth: The African Experience, by Michael T. Hadjimichael, Michael Nowak, Robert Sharer, and Amor Tahari. 1996.

142. Quasi-Fiscal Operations of Public Financial Institutions, by G.A. Mackenzie and Peter Stella. 1996.

141. Monetary and Exchange System Reforms in China: An Experiment in Gradualism, by Hassanali Mehran, Marc Quintyn, Tom Nordman, and Bernard Laurens. 1996.

140. Government Reform in New Zealand, by Graham C. Scott. 1996.

139. Reinvigorating Growth in Developing Countries: Lessons from Adjustment Policies in Eight Economies, by David Goldsbrough, Sharmini Coorey, Louis Dicks-Mireaux, Balazs Horvath, Kalpana Kochhar, Mauro Mecagni, Erik Offerdal, and Jianping Zhou. 1996.

138. Aftermath of the CFA Franc Devaluation, by Jean A.P. Clément, with Johannes Mueller, Stéphane Cossé, and Jean Le Dem. 1996.

137. The Lao People's Democratic Republic: Systemic Transformation and Adjustment, edited by Ichiro Otani and Chi Do Pham. 1996.

136. Jordan: Strategy for Adjustment and Growth, edited by Edouard Maciejewski and Ahsan Mansur. 1996.

135. Vietnam: Transition to a Market Economy, by John R. Dodsworth, Erich Spitäller, Michael Braulke, Keon Hyok Lee, Kenneth Miranda, Christian Mulder, Hisanobu Shishido, and Krishna Srinivasan. 1996.

134. India: Economic Reform and Growth, by Ajai Chopra, Charles Collyns, Richard Hemming, and Karen Parker with Woosik Chu and Oliver Fratzscher. 1995.

133. Policy Experiences and Issues in the Baltics, Russia, and Other Countries of the Former Soviet Union, edited by Daniel A. Citrin and Ashok K. Lahiri. 1995.

132. Financial Fragilities in Latin America: The 1980s and 1990s, by Liliana Rojas-Suárez and Steven R. Weisbrod. 1995.

131. Capital Account Convertibility: Review of Experience and Implications for IMF Policies, by staff teams headed by Peter J. Quirk and Owen Evans. 1995.

130. Challenges to the Swedish Welfare State, by Desmond Lachman, Adam Bennett, John H. Green, Robert Hagemann, and Ramana Ramaswamy. 1995.

129. IMF Conditionality: Experience Under Stand-By and Extended Arrangements. Part II: Background Papers. Susan Schadler, Editor, with Adam Bennett, Maria Carkovic, Louis Dicks-Mireaux, Mauro Mecagni, James H.J. Morsink, and Miguel A. Savastano. 1995.

128. IMF Conditionality: Experience Under Stand-By and Extended Arrangements. Part I: Key Issues and Findings, by Susan Schadler, Adam Bennett, Maria Carkovic, Louis Dicks-Mireaux, Mauro Mecagni, James H.J. Morsink, and Miguel A. Savastano. 1995.

127. Road Maps of the Transition: The Baltics, the Czech Republic, Hungary, and Russia, by Biswajit Banerjee, Vincent Koen, Thomas Krueger, Mark S. Lutz, Michael Marrese, and Tapio O. Saavalainen. 1995.

126. The Adoption of Indirect Instruments of Monetary Policy, by a staff team headed by William E. Alexander, Tomás J.T. Baliño, and Charles Enoch. 1995.

**Note:** For information on the title and availability of Occasional Papers not listed, please consult the IMF Publications Catalog or contact IMF Publication Services.